HAPPY BIRTHDAY

A PLAY IN TWO ACTS

by
Anita Loos

SAMUEL FRENCH

New York   Los Angeles   Toronto

In love and gratitude

to

HELEN HAYES

"Happy Birthday" was first produced by Richard Rodgers and Oscar Hammerstein 2nd at the Broadhurst Theatre in New York City on November 1, 1946. The play was directed by Joshua Logan, the scenery was designed and lighted by Jo Mielziner and the costumes were designed by Lucinda Ballard. Helen Hayes headed the cast which was as follows:

(In order of their appearance)

GAIL	Margaret Irving
GLORIOUS	Musa Williams
DAD MALONE	Thomas Heaphy
GABE	Charles Gordon
BELLA	Florence Sundstrom
HERMAN	Jack Diamond
MYRTLE	Jacqueline Paige
JUNE	Jean Bellows
ADDIE	Helen Hayes
MAUDE	Lorraine Miller
DON	Dort Clark
THE JUDGE	Ralph Theodore
PAUL	Louis Jean Heydt
POLICEMAN	Philip Dakin
TOT	Enid Markey
EMMA	Grace Valentine
MANUEL	Philip Gordon
MARGOT	Eleanor Boleyn
BERT	James Livingston
MR. BEMIS	Robert Burton
MR. NANINO	Harry Kingston

The action takes place in the
Jersey Mecca Cocktail Bar in Newark, N. J.

ACT I

. Late afternoon

INTERMISSION

ACT II

Immediately afterwards .

Incidental Music by Robert Russell Bennett

"I Haven't Got a Worry in the World"
by Richard Rodgers and Oscar Hammerstein 2nd

ACT ONE

ACT ONE

SCENE: *The setting shows us the Jersey Mecca cocktail lounge in a section of Newark which is adjacent to a business district and also near a neighborhood of modest homes. The decor of the Mecca bears out its title and, although somewhat dingy, puts up a brave show of being "Oriental." On the walls are several old photographs and cartoon drawings of "famous" patrons of the house who might be local politicians and figures of the sporting world. Spanning the Center of the ceiling is an arch on which is written in fancy lettering:*

THROUGH THESE PORTALS
PASS THE NICEST PEOPLE
IN NEWARK

To an extent the motto is true, for the regular patrons of the Jersey Mecca are searchers after beauty—sensitive souls not content with life-as-it-is.

The scene is set on a platform above the regular stage. The platform has a gentle slope which provides the audience with a clear view of the whole stage. The bar [with three stools] is at Left. At the back wall Center is a streamlined and decorative juke box, a piano Right of it and a microphone Left. Tables with chairs dot the floor space, in the Center of which is a small area for dancing. Tables: No. 1 down Left; No. 2 Left Center; No. 3 Right Center; No. 4 down Right; No. 5 up Center; No. 6 up Left; No. 7 up Right. There is a coat rack up Right Center and a telephone Right Center on wall.

The proprietress of the Jersey Mecca is GAIL HOSMER, a woman of about forty-five. GAIL makes it a point to be well-

3

groomed and is indeed a handsome figure in a full-blown manner.

The waiter is a gray-haired old boy of sixty-five, DAD MALONE. DAD *never had a drink in his life and is a militant moralist wherever morality can be expressed in high-sounding words and fancy precepts. He is fully aware that a non-drinking bar waiter is an anomaly and makes the most of it. The bartender [* HERMAN *] seems to pay no attention to anything but the filling of orders which he generally hears before they are relayed to him by* DAD. *This makes for efficiency and speed in service while, at the same time, it gives* HERMAN *an air of being rather remote.·*

The only customers at the rise of the Curtain are a YOUNG PAIR *who sit in moody silence Right Center at table No. 3, and a nondescript* GIRL *who sits alone up Left, table No. 6, casually playing solitaire.*

AT RISE: *At the rise of the Curtain,* GAIL *is seated at table Right, table No. 4 [on which there is a table cloth], just finishing a sandwich and a cup of coffee.* DAD *stands near the bar glancing over the evening paper.* HERMAN *leans on the mahogany bar, day-dreaming.*

There is a moment of silence which is thrown into relief by the yowling of a heavy wind.

During this period, the colored girl-of-all-work, who cleans up the place and helps serve during rush hours, has entered from the kitchen regions up Left to bring GAIL *a fresh cup of coffee and remove the remains of her snack. She bears the peculiar name of* GLORIOUS *and being both religious and uninhibited bursts forth from time to time with snatches of hymns which she sings in swing rhythm. She now intones: "Ain't it a shame to sin on Sunday."*

GAIL. See what the weather looks like now, Dad, will you?

[DAD *goes to the door.*]

GLORIOUS. [*To* GAIL—*as she glances toward door.*] Uhm, uhm, Mis' Hosmer! It's as dark out there as all creation.

GAIL. Yeah. [*Glancing at time.*] Only a little past five-thirty and you'd think it was midnight.

DAD. [*As he returns to bar from looking out the door.*] Don't seem like there'd ever be any let-up to that rain, Gail.

GAIL. An April "shower"! April whirlpool would be more to the point. [*Rises.*]

GLORIOUS. You said it, Mis' Hosmer. Guess there won't be nobody in tonight but the regulars. [*Crossing up Left to kitchen.*]

GAIL. That's right.

[*During the above the* GIRL *at table up Left playing solitaire rises, goes to put a nickel in the juke box and returns to her game. This* GIRL *has a strangely relaxed attitude as if she were alone and in her own home. Now* GABE DARCY, *the young man of the seated couple at table Right Center, No. 3, speaks.*]

GABE. Ssst, Dad! [*As* DAD *approaches he addresses his companion* BELLA.] What'll you have this time, Monkey?

BELLA. The same.

DAD. Okay, Miss Lane. [*Turns to* GABE.] And you, Mr. Darcy?

GABE. The same for me.

DAD. Yes, Sir. [*He goes to the bar.*]

BELLA. Gabe. This lawyer you dug up. You sure he can get that divorce from your wife in time?

GABE. You mean before—?

BELLA. I mean before it's too late!

GABE. Of course, Monkey. Why Judge Hollister ain't just a lawyer. He used to be a judge. You've got to call him "Your Honor."

BELLA. Hollister! Wasn't his honor impeached that time for getting the jury drunk?

GABE. Well—Judges can get in trouble just like anybody else.

BELLA. They can't get in trouble like I'm in trouble.

GABE. [Seeing somebody enter; crossing to door.] Who's that?—Oh!

BELLA. Get that wind, will you?

GABE. [Handing her drink.] Here you are, Monkey, take it easy.

[At this point another of the regular customers has entered by the name of JUNE. She is the type of girl who for a good time or a drink will go with anybody.]

JUNE. Hello, Gail. [Crosses Left Center.]

GAIL. —Well, hello dear! Some weather out there isn't it?

[Crosses down to table Left, No. 1.]

JUNE. [Taking off coat.] Yeah. Hello, Dad!

DAD. [In sad reproval of her.] Good evening.

[GLORIOUS enters up Left to JUNE.]

JUNE. How're, Gloria?

GLORIOUS. Don't call me Gloria, Miss June. My name is Glorious after the Glorious word of the Lamb. [She takes coat to coatrack.]

JUNE. I always thought it was singular; sorry. [*To* GAIL, *as she glances about.*] Ain't Don here yet?

GAIL. [*With a start.*] You don't mean my Don? [*Looks at* JUNE.]

JUNE. I sure do. His boat docked at the navy yard this morning. [*To* HERMAN.] That's right, Herman, and heavy on the gin. [*Sits on stool No. 2.*]

GAIL. How'd you *know* Don's boat got in?

JUNE. [*Taking out telegram.*] He sent me this.

GAIL. —Thanks.

[GABE *goes up to play juke box.*]

JUNE. [*Raising her glass.*] Well, Gail, here's hoping our sailor boy turns up sober and single.

GAIL. You said it, Sister.

GLORIOUS. There's one thing about a bad night like this one, Mis' Hosmer. If we don't have no customers we don't have no trouble with the cops. [*Laughs.*]

GAIL. That's right.

JUNE. What's the matter, Gail? Police after you again?

GAIL. Yeah! Everything that ever happens in here gets reported.

DAD. And the way things get exaggerated. I wish I could meet that guy that's putting in raps against us.

GAIL. Like as not it's some female. The worst bluenoses are.

JUNE. Why don't you get yourself another racket, Gail?

GAIL. Give up the Jersey Mecca?

JUNE. If it's such a pain in the neck?

[GABE *puts nickel in juke box and it starts playing.*]

GAIL. Did it ever occur to you, you get sort of fond of a place in eighteen years?—If I ever do sell the little trap, it'll be when Don leaves the Merchant Marine—so's he can settle down.

[BELLA *goes up to* GABE *at juke box.*]

JUNE. Settle down? You and Don, eh?

GAIL. Sure! Why shouldn't he live somewhere with his mother—in a nice home?

JUNE. Supposing he wants to get married?

GAIL. When he wants to get married he'll tell me.

JUNE. Yeah! Well he telegraphed *me*.

GAIL. He knows I don't like telegrams.

[*At which point* ADDIE *enters Right gingerly and seats herself near the door at table No. 4. She has a bandage on her right wrist.*]

GLORIOUS. [*Up Right at piano—to* GAIL *indicating* ADDIE.] Ssst, Mis' Hosmer.

[*She exits up Left.*]

GAIL. [*To* DAD *indicating* ADDIE.] Dad!

DAD. [DAD *turns, sees* ADDIE *and reacts amazed.*] Well—for Pete's sake!

GAIL. Who is it?

DAD. The girl I rent my room from. My landlady. For Pete's sake.

GAIL. [*Disgusted.*] Do you mean Homer Bemis' daughter?

DAD. Yeah!

GAIL. I don't want to see that drunk Homer Bemis in here, or any member of his family. If she wants to go on a toot, tell her to try some other place.

DAD. Toot! Why, Addie's never had a drink in her life. She works in the library.

GAIL. Well, this ain't a little Gypsy Tea Kettle, either. Tell her to run along.

DAD. I'll see what she wants.

[*As he crosses to* ADDIE—GAIL *exits up Left for a moment.*]

ADDIE. [*Revealing her discomfort over her surroundings.*] Good evening, Mr. Malone!

DAD. What on earth are you doing here, Addie?

ADDIE. [*Evading his question.*] I—I'm not in a place like this from choice, Mr. Malone!

DAD. I can't get over it! You in a saloon, Addie! Why I've heard you say a thousand times you'd never set foot in one.

ADDIE. [*With a note of desperation.*] I wouldn't be here to-night, except I've got to see—Mr. Bishop. It's imperative.

DAD. Paul Bishop?

ADDIE. Yes.

DAD. But he isn't here.

ADDIE. He'll be here! The watchman at the bank said he was on his way.

DAD. What do you want to see Mr. Bishop about?

ADDIE. It's something personal.

DAD. What?

ADDIE. [*Anguished.*] Oh please don't ask me. It's something so—so humiliating.—I just can't talk about it.

DAD. [*Very kindly.*] Look, Honey, Mrs. Hosmer told me to tell you you'd better run along.

ADDIE. She did? [*Downright importunate.*] Oh, it's desperately important!—Please don't make me go.

[*By which time* GAIL *has returned and, mildly interested, starts toward them.*]

DAD. [*Deeply mystified.*] But I'm not the boss here, Addie. Mrs. Hosmer's the one you'll have to talk to.

[*Forcing a desperate smile,* ADDIE *turns to face* GAIL.]

GAIL. [*With a trace of kindly interest.*] So you're Homer Bemis' daughter?

ADDIE. Why, yes. And you must be Mrs. Hosmer. [*Rises.*]

GAIL. That's right.

ADDIE. [*Pathetically inept.*] I knew, because my father's told me so many lovely things about you.

GAIL. [*Amused.*] Wait a moment, Miss Bemis. I know what your father thinks of me and he knows what I think of him.

ADDIE. [*Reacts with despair.*] Oh dear!

DAD. Addie wants to wait and see Mr. Bishop, Gail, but if her old man came in here with a snootful there'd be hell to pay.

ADDIE. But Papa's—

DAD. When he's like that, and gets one look at her, it's like a red rag to a bull.

GAIL. In that case, Miss Bemis, you'd better run on home. It's too bad, but I'm in wrong with the Law as it is.

ADDIE. Oh, Mrs. Hosmer,—please! Papa won't be coming in. He's way down town. He phoned just now—before I quit work at the library. [*Turning back to* DAD.] And if Mr. Bishop doesn't show up soon—I won't risk waiting.

GAIL. Wish I could afford to take the chance, Miss, I'm sorry.

ADDIE. [*Despairing and about to give up.*] Oh, don't apologize. Please. [*She goes to door, then turning, makes one more desperate effort.*] I think it's very worthy of you, Mrs. Hosmer, to want to keep your place refined.

GAIL. [*Graciously.*] Well, thanks. And you know how it is these days, with folks inclined to be rowdy. And when some noisy bum shows up—I'm sorry. I didn't mean—

ADDIE. Oh, I understand. I know Papa has his faults and I'd be the last to condone them. But he's awfully particular. And the fact that he comes here often—well—it shows you only serve the best.

DAD. Addie!

GAIL. [ADDIE's *flattery to the Mecca causing her to overlook* DAD's *exclamation.*] Why, thanks, Miss Bemis.

ADDIE. I'll warrant it isn't easy to keep your standards high with things as they are now.

GAIL. No, it isn't.

ADDIE. All the more credit to you, Mrs. Hosmer.

GAIL. Thanks.

ADDIE. [ADDIE *picks up her raincoat. To* GAIL, *making a big issue of the wounded wrist.*] Could you help me on, please, with my raincoat?

GAIL. [*As she obliges.*] Why, sure, young lady. How'd you hurt yourself?

ADDIE. It's nothing. But it's awfully sweet and kind of you to ask. [*Then indicating a twinge of pain in her wrist appears about to faint.*]

DAD. [*Worried.*] Your old man's on the rampage *tonight*, isn't he?

ADDIE. It's nothing. I put the bandage on more as a protection.

GAIL. Take it easy there. Say that hurts, doesn't it?

ADDIE. [*Clasping her wrist from pain.*] It's nothing. Rainy weather makes things seem worse, you know. It'll be all right in a moment. [*She glances at the chair down Right.*]

GAIL. Maybe you'd better sit down a moment.

ADDIE. [*With alacrity she sits.*] Oh, thanks.

DAD. Gail!

GAIL. The poor kid needs a shot of something. [*To* ADDIE.] What'll I make it, Miss Bemis, whiskey?

ADDIE. [*Suspicious.*] Oh no—oh dear no—I never drink.

GAIL. A coke or something?

ADDIE. —a glass of water would be refreshing.

[GABE *puts nickel in juke box and he and* BELLA *start dancing.*]

GAIL. [*Touched by the modesty of her request.*] Okay!

[GAIL *goes to bar for it.*]

DAD. Addie, what are you up to tonight?

ADDIE. Up to?

DAD. Does Mr. Bishop know you?

ADDIE. Well I should hope so. He sees me every week—when I make my deposits through his window at the bank.—He knows me very well.

DAD. But, Addie—

ADDIE. Please!—

GAIL. [*Returning with glass of water.*] Here you are, little lady—one on the city.

ADDIE. —"one on the"—? Oh! Oh! how clever of you! "One on the city." [*She now starts to take off her galoshes revealing the one note of vanity in her entire make-up—a pair of shoes strapped around the ankles.*] It's so darling of you to let me stay here until Mr. Bishop comes—It's so dear of you.

GAIL. [*Uncomfortably.*] But, uh, wait a minute. I uh—

ADDIE. "One on the city." I'll have to remember that!

GAIL. Well, it's just a gag. [*Giving up. Notes* ADDIE's *shoes.*] My, what pretty shoes, dear.

ADDIE. Oh, thanks. That's sweet and kind of you.

GAIL. They look expensive, too.

ADDIE. They are. It's my one folly.

GAIL. What do you think of my little "trap," Miss Bemis?

ADDIE. [*Looking about, speaks with an awe which seems like sheer hyperbole.*] Oh, you shouldn't call it that, even in fun. A place with the reputation this has.

GAIL. Is that a crack, Miss Bemis?

ADDIE. [*Quickly, looking about the room.*] Oh no. It's so—colorful! And such lovely customers—

[BELLA *and* GABE *are in each other's arms and* JUNE *is tossing off a drink at the bar.*]

GAIL. [*Convinced* ADDIE *is on the level, once more expands.*] Yeah. [*Indicating motto over the arch.*] How'd you like my motto there—over the arch?

ADDIE. [*Rises, reading it inspiredly.*] "Through these portals pass the nicest people in Newark!"

GAIL. [*With awe.*] Say, you made that sound like something.

ADDIE. That's only because it says the truth! [*Sits down Right; picks up a paper which turns out to be a copy of Racing Form.*]

GAIL. Thanks. That's right, honey, pick yourself a horse.

[*At this point a young lady enters. She is the neighborhood beauty and the receptionist of the Orchid Beauty Shop. Her name is* MAUDE CARSON. MAUDE'S *dialogue indicates the crashing type of stupidity which insists on being heard and, because of her beauty, is heard with lenience. She carries a copy of "Good Housekeeping."*] Good evening, dear.

MAUDE. How'd-a-doody? [*As she shakes her umbrella at Center.*] This rain! Well! It's—wet!

GAIL. You said it, Honey! Here give me that. [*Helps her off with coat and puts it on rack.*]

MAUDE. Thanky, ma'am. [*Then looking about the room with a disappointed little move.*] Oh! Isn't Mr. Bishop here yet?

[*The mention of* BISHOP *causes* ADDIE *to look at* MAUDE.]

GAIL. Not yet! There's another young lady waiting for him.

MAUDE. [*Surprised and a little jealous.*] —There—is?

GAIL. Yeah. [*Noting* ADDIE *is watching them gestures surreptitiously and speaks in a low tone.*] That one—over there.

MAUDE. [*Looking at* ADDIE *makes no effort to disguise her feelings about her or lower her voice.*] You don't mean she's waiting for Mr. Bishop?

GAIL. Yeah. She's from the library. It must be some sort of a contribution—or—you know—a bite of some kind.

MAUDE. [*With unconcealed contempt.*] Well! It certainly must be!

GAIL. Sit down, honey. Mr. Bishop won't be long—not with you as a magnet.

MAUDE. Oh! Thanky two times! [*She goes Left Center to table No. 2.*]

DAD. [*Crossing to her*] Would you care to order now, Miss?
MAUDE. No, thanky, I'll wait. [*With a sigh.*] Mr. Bishop never knows when he's going to get out of that bank. Now with my job, I leave at five-thirty if the Orchid Beauty Shop collapses. But with Mr. Bishop—well—I just give him up and say [*With a shrug.*] Che sara, sara. [*Sits Left of Table No. 2.*]

GAIL. That's Italian, isn't it?

MAUDE. Yes I picked it up from Mr. Nanino. He's my boss.

JUNE. What does it mean?

MAUDE. Oh nothing—it's Italian.

[*Whistle off Right.*]

JUNE. [*As she descends from bar stool.*] If that ain't Don, it's a reasonable facsimile!

[*As* GAIL *turns rigidly to face the door,* JUNE *starts toward it.* DON *enters in uniform of the Merchant Marine. The embodiment of sexy roughness, he is pretty wet from the rain.* GLORIOUS *enters up Left from kitchen; crosses Center.*]

DON. Get out of my way, Dizzy—I want my Mom.

[*He pushes* JUNE *away and she loses her balance, joggles* ADDIE'S *chair.*]

JUNE. [*To* ADDIE *as she steadies herself.*] Sorry, lady.

ADDIE. [*Sweetly—with her smile.*] —It's all right.

GAIL. [*Overly casual—keeps him off.*] —Hello, Don!

DON. [*Crossing Center to* GAIL.] Don't give us that "Hello Don" stuff, Mom! Slip us a kiss.

[*He takes her in his arms and kisses her with all the warmth one might accord a sweetheart. The kiss does its job well and* GAIL *melts.*]

GAIL. [*Holding him close.*] Donny boy! Gee I'm glad to see you. [*Alarmed pulls off his wet jacket.*] Here! Get out of that jacket! It's soaking!

DON. You'll be too, hugging me like that!

GAIL. Oh!

DON. Anywhere she's at, June, she's the prettiest! [*Crosses Right to* JUNE.]

JUNE. [*Trying to conceal her jealousy.*] I wouldn't give two pins for a guy that wasn't stuck on his mother!

DON. You're as jealous as hell and you know it. [*He shoves her Up Right with a slap on her rear.*]

GAIL. [*A trace bitterly.*] She doesn't have to be jealous! You wired her—not me.

DON. [*With a big impudent grin, puts foot on Right Center chair.*] I did that to get your goat, Mom!

GAIL. [*Her heart leaping for joy—crossing down Right Center to* DON.] Don! Did you!

[GLORIOUS *crosses down Left Center.*]

DON. Sure! [*Spotting* GLORIOUS.] Hello there, "small, dark and handsome"!

GLORIOUS. [*Moving in.*] Hello, Mr. Don! Gee you sure look divine.

DON. [*Grinning.*] Sharp as a jackknife, eh? [*At which point he spots* ADDIE'S *critical gaze on him and addresses her.*] Some other night, Babe! [*As* ADDIE *reacts, covering her repulsion he turns to* DAD *and* HERMAN, *crossing Left Center.*] How you doin', fish ears?

DAD. Fine.

DON. [*Spotting* MAUDE.] The joint's on fire! [*He barks sexily at her, crossing up Center.*] Say, Mom! What is it with that mike? And the piano?

GAIL. [*Follows* DON.] Some friends of mine—a little song and dance team—I'm letting them try their act out here to-night.

DON. [*To* JUNE.] She's everybody's pal, she is!

GAIL. Pal nothing! That's how I get a floor show for free.

DON. [*Tries out the mike—singing through it.*] "I'm just a prisoner of love."

GAIL. Better fix Don a hot toddy, Herman.

DON. Make it a double whiskey sour, Pal. [*Crossing to bar.*]

GAIL. [*To* HERMAN *insistently.*] Good and hot.

DON. [*Sitting at bar with* JUNE—*in remonstration.*] Aw gee, Mom! [*To* HERMAN.] Double whiskey sour, Pal.

[*At this point the door is opened by a middle-aged man who enters in a gust of wind and rain. He is* JUDGE HOLLISTER. *He carries a big briefcase and is very tight.* BELLA *gives a start and nudges* GABE.]

JUDGE. Greetings, madam!

BELLA. [*Moving down with* GABE.] Is that the Judge?

GABE. Yeah!

GAIL. [*At door.*] Good evening, Your Honor!

JUDGE. Greetings, gentlemen!

BELLA. His Honor's loaded!

GABE. Sssh!

GAIL. [*Pointing to table—crossing Center with* JUDGE.] Would you like to sit there this evening, Judge?

JUDGE. No thanks. I have some important clients waiting for me. [*Sees* GABE.] —Oh! There you are, Mr. Darcy.

GABE. [*Crossing to* JUDGE.] H'yah, Judge. Meet Bella Lane.

BELLA. —Hello, Your Honor.

JUDGE. Miss Lane.

DAD. [*Crossing to Left of* JUDGE.] Well Judge, how about a nice cup of hot coffee now?

JUDGE. I've been drinking coffee all afternoon. [*Stopping to burp.*] So make it Bourbon.

[DAD *looks at* GAIL *for permission to refuse the* JUDGE.]

GAIL. Go get it for His Honor, Dad. [DAD *goes to bar.*] It's my theory to let a customer gauge his own capacity, Judge, if he's a gentleman.

JUDGE. Spoken like a scholar and a. lady. This, madam, is a sanitarium for the spirit.

GABE. Get the Judge, Bella.

GAIL. Gee that's nice. A "sanitarium for the spirit."

JUDGE. Madam, I only spoke what is in the heart of everybody in this room. [DAD *returns with the* JUDGE's *drink.* ADDIE, *in a sudden gesture, slams down her glass.*] You know what I mean, don't you, madam? Always go to a solitary drinker for the truth! [*Crossing to table No. 3 Right Center.*] It is in such places that shy natures become capable of expression, expand into good fellowship and grow mellow. [*To* ADDIE.] Am I right, madam? [*Sits Right of table.*]

ADDIE. [*With superb hypocrisy.*] Oh—yes.

JUDGE. Then let me match my golden Bourbon to your pellucid gin. Bottoms up! [*He drinks then turns to* GABE *and* BELLA *who have sat at Right Center table.*] Children, I bring you glad tidings.

GABE. What did I tell you, Monkey!

JUDGE. I have a full report from Sam Tuttle, my colleague in Las Vegas. [*Trying to extract some papers from briefcase.*] "Honest Sam" they call him in Nevada.

BELLA. Yeah, but what does he say?

JUDGE. Mr. Darcy, if your wife can leave for Las Vegas at once, Sam guarantees her a divorce in just six weeks.

BELLA. Yeah—and what's it going to cost?

GABE. Yeah, Judge, this divorce has got to be cheap!

BELLA. And it's got to be quick too!

JUDGE. [*Taking envelope and showing it to* BELLA.] Well, here it is.

BELLA. Two hundred and forty-three dollars and eighty cents!

GABE. Gee!

JUDGE. Well—there's the round trip bus fare.

BELLA. But we can't get hold of that much dough by December.

JUDGE. December? What's December got to do with it?

BELLA. Well—uh—

JUDGE. Miss Lane! Are you going to have a baby?

GABE. Ssh, Judge!

BELLA. Pipe down, Your Honor.

JUDGE. Don't worry, Miss Lane. Your secret is absolutely safe with me.

GABE. Let's move over to that other table, Judge.

[*As they start to move* ADDIE *sees* BELLA *for the first time.* JUDGE *and* GABE *move up Right to table No. 7.*]

ADDIE. [*Rises.*] Hello, Bella! [BELLA *turns and looks at her without recognition.*] It's Addie—Addie Bemis. [*Crosses toward* BELLA.]

BELLA. —Oh hello, Addie. I didn't know you. Well, I guess we've all got to get old sometime, don't we!—I didn't mean—

ADDIE. [*In a sweet attempt to erase* BELLA'S *faux-pas.*] That's all right, Bella! You still joke just like when you were the kid next door.

BELLA. Yeah. Oh, sure.

ADDIE. You're as lovely as ever, Bella. You've hardly changed at all.

BELLA. [*With a somewhat wry attempt at humor.*] 'Spose that's from the quiet life I've been leading. [*Anxious to get away from her—as she backs away.*] Glad to of seen you, Addie. You're looking great! [*Crosses up to join* GABE *and* JUDGE.]

ADDIE. Thanks, Bella. That's sweet of you. [*Sits again.*]

[*The* GIRL *has gone to juke box and put a nickel in, playing "Melancholy Baby." At that moment* PAUL BISHOP *enters. Cashier in the neighborhood bank, he is about thirty-five—a fine hearty fellow, fond of life, fun loving, extremely popular with men and as in the case of so many 100% males a complete bungler where women are concerned. There is a certain nervous quality about* PAUL'S *high spirits which makes them seem a trace hectic and even unhealthy, but of this he is unaware being superbly an extrovert.*]

GAIL and DAD. How are you, Mr. Bishop? How'd a 'do, Honey?

[GAIL *crosses to meet* PAUL.]

PAUL. [*Crossing Center.*] Hello, folks! [*Anxiously addressing the nearest of the above characters.*] Is Miss Carson—

MAUDE. [*Speaking up in arch reproval.*] *Miss Carson's* been waiting here a long, *long time,* Mr. Bishop!

PAUL. [*Crossing to* MAUDE.] I'm sorry, Maude. But I got hung up at the bank.

MAUDE. *I* understand, Paulie.

PAUL. [*To* GAIL *heartily.*] Isn't she a sweetheart! [*He starts to take off his coat, fumbling a bit in his nervousness.*]

GAIL. [*Beginning to study him.*] I'll say so. Here let me help you off with that.

PAUL. Gee, Gail, you spoil a guy!

GAIL. [*Beginning to study him closely.*] Nothing can spoil you, darlin', but I don't like the way you look.

[*Takes coat and hat and hands them to* GLORIOUS *to hang on rack.*]

PAUL. Who me?

GAIL. Yeah. Nervous and all.

PAUL. [*Laughing it off.*] I'm swell. You're the worrying type, Honey, that's it.

ADDIE. [*With extreme humility half rises from her seat to address* PAUL.] Oh Mr. Bish—

[*She gets no further, for Paul in his eagerness to join his girl does not see her and* ADDIE *is left in an ungraceful half standing position.* GAIL *goes down to* ADDIE.]

PAUL. Hey, Dad! How about a drink.

[DAD *down to* PAUL, *who sits above table No. 2.*]

GAIL. [*To* ADDIE.] Sit down, dear. I'll get him for you.

ADDIE. There's no hurry *yet.* Leave them alone a minute.

GAIL. Okay, Honey.

DAD. [*Approaching table.*] What'll it be, folks?

MAUDE. A Pink Lady please.

PAUL. An Old-fashioned.

DAD. The usual eh! [*He goes to get drinks.*]

ADDIE. [*To* GAIL.] A Pink Lady! What's that?

GAIL. A drink.

ADDIE. A pretty name—"Pink Lady."

GAIL. Yeah—It's pink.

ADDIE. [*Taking her courage in both hands.*] He isn't—in love with her, is he?

GAIL. Figure it out for yourself.

ADDIE. I suppose she's in love with him.

GAIL. Why not? I could go for him myself. Couldn't you?

ADDIE. Why—I—I—

GAIL. Okay, Sister. You've answered me.

[*She moves away leaving* ADDIE *to her own desperate reaction. For, up to this point* ADDIE *has been unaware that she is in love.*]

ADDIE. Oh, no—no!

PAUL. Now tell me, how'd your interview with the boss work out today? Did you tell him you were quitting?

MAUDE. Well a funny thing happened, Paul! I was just going to tell Vittorio about quitting when he said he was going to promote me to the main shop just off Park Avenue and—

PAUL. So he's Vittorio now!

MAUDE. We girls all use Nanino's first name behind his back.

PAUL. That guy's stuck on you, isn't he?

MAUDE. Paul!

PAUL. You're stalling again! [*Rises and crosses to Center.*]

MAUDE. Where are you going?

PAUL. I'm going to phone Nanino to come down here and have a drink with us.

MAUDE. Are you out of your mind? Why if he saw me here with you he'd— [*Rises; crosses to* PAUL.]

PAUL. He'd *what?* And what of it?

MAUDE. Can't you understand?—There's a rule about us girls being seen in public drinking. He'd make a scene. And he's not sensible like you, Paulie. He's emotional. He's from the South of Italy.

PAUL. Say—you're not stuck on him, are you?

MAUDE. [*Hurt to the core starts to cry.*] Paulie! If you can't trust me, maybe I ought to find it out before I—

[*Crosses back to their table.*]

PAUL. Don't cry, Honey. I can't stand to see you cry. I'm sorry.

MAUDE. Well! That's better—better.

[*She wrinkles her nose and holds it up to be kissed. He obliges—they sit as before.*]

GLORIOUS. [*Singing—to* GAIL—*in warning*] Somebody's knocking at your door—Somebody's knocking at your door—

[*At which point a* POLICE OFFICER *makes his entrance, and remains at the door.* GAIL *sees* POLICEMAN *and reacts concernedly.*]

GAIL. [*Approaching him.*] Good evening, Officer. How about a nice hot cup of coffee on a blustery night?

POLICEMAN. No, thanks. D'you know a guy in this neighborhood named Homer Bemis?

[ADDIE *gives a start.* DAD *galvanizes.* NOBODY *else pays any attention as* POLICEMAN *looks around the room.*]

GAIL. [*With an uneasy glance at* ADDIE.] —I think I know the guy you mean.

POLICEMAN. You'd better report to the station if he comes in here. [*He starts out.*]

DAD. [*Speaking up.*] What's he done now, Officer?

POLICEMAN. Nothing yet, but we just heard from Headquarters he's out looking for trouble. [*With which he goes back into the storm.*]

[*As* GAIL *turns toward* ADDIE *with concern,* ADDIE *rises uncomfortably.*]

ADDIE. I'll have my talk with Mr. Bishop right away, Mrs. Hosmer, and then I'll just slip out quietly. [*Resolutely she makes her way to* PAUL'S *table and stands there hoping he'll look up. But, engrossed in* MAUDE, *he doesn't. She clears her throat nervously.* GAIL *goes up Right then to bar.*] Good evening, Mr. Bishop. [*As* PAUL *glances up it's obvious he doesn't recognize her.*] —I'm Addie Bemis. Perhaps you remember seeing me at the bank.

PAUL. [*Rising politely.*] Oh! Oh, yes, Mrs. Bemis. [*Being single* ADDIE *reacts to the "Mrs."*] This is Miss Carson.

ADDIE. Good evening!

MAUDE. How'd doody?

ADDIE. I'm awfully sorry to interrupt your tête-à-tête, Miss Carson, but I would like to have a word alone with Mr. Bishop—if you wouldn't mind of course.

MAUDE. Not in the least, Mrs. Bemis.

ADDIE. It's about the bank, so you needn't worry.

MAUDE. [*With such a lack of jealousy as to be an insult.*]
Oh, I'm not worried.

ADDIE. [*To* PAUL.] —Could we—go over— [*She gestures to
table No. 4 where she has been sitting.*]

PAUL. [*Wondering, yet gracious.*] Sure! [*To* MAUDE.] 'Scuse
me a minute, Honey. [*He follows* ADDIE *over to table. En
route to table.*] I have to apologize for not recognizing you,
Mrs. Bemis. But— [*Finding he is making matters worse,
starts to flounder.*] —but—well—the light in here—it's—

ADDIE. You don't have to apologize, Mr. Bishop. Everybody
says your politeness is the biggest asset the bank's got. And
I *so* agree.

[*They sit;* ADDIE *Left;* PAUL *Right.*]

PAUL. Now you embarrass me!

ADDIE. But it's true. You always seem to take such an interest, whether people are important—like the Mayor or
somebody—or unimportant—like me.

PAUL. [*Revealing his keen interest in his job.*] It's my theory
that everyone who comes into the bank is important, Mrs.
Bemis.

ADDIE. [*With a trace of arch criticism.*] If that's your theory,
Mr. Bishop, I'm *Miss* Bemis.

PAUL. Sorry! [*With charm, but at the same time anxious to
be back with* MAUDE.] What's on your mind, Miss Bemis?

ADDIE. [*Her humility taking on a rather coy quality.*] Well—
it's—it's a little hard to know how to begin. [*Hesitates a*

brief moment—then.] You see I have a problem, Mr.
Bishop. It isn't very hard to handle except where other
people are concerned, but something's come up today that
puts you in—in the disagreeable spot of being one of the
other people.

[GAIL *goes to* MAUDE'S *table, sits and chats with her.*]

PAUL. [*Surprised.*] —Me?

ADDIE. [*Nods.*] You see, Mr. Bishop, it's like this. [*She
settles back quite comfortably to tell her story—a fact which
causes* GAIL *some uneasiness.*] I have a father who's—well,
he's pretty headstrong. And when he gets hold of an idea
that upsets him he's—rather hard to handle. [*At which point,
noting* GAIL'S *uneasiness, she sits up, as if ready to leave at
any moment and* GAIL *relaxes.*] For instance, Papa's got the
idea lately that I'm planning to leave home. I mean—he—he
thinks it's over some man.

PAUL. That's ridiculous!

ADDIE. [*Stabbed.*] Oh yes—I suppose it is ridiculous, isn't it?

PAUL. [*Trying to make things right.*] Oh no. I didn't mean
that. I mean you're not the type to lose your head over a
man, are you?

ADDIE. [*Gazing at him.*] Oh no— [*Then—anxious to change
the subject.*] You see, Mr. Bishop, there's a secret I've been
keeping from Papa. When I opened that account with you
at the bank, I didn't tell him about it. Because, well—because
he wouldn't like it. I didn't think he'd ever find out—because
the money came from extra work I've been doing on Sundays and holidays.

PAUL. [*With interest and a trace touched.*] Sundays and
holidays? When d'you have your fun?

ADDIE. [*Mysteriously.*] Oh—I have my "resources"!

PAUL. [*A trace curiously.*] You do?

ADDIE. Yes. Reading and—and piano. I buy the new songs as they come out and learn them.

PAUL. To entertain your friends, eh?

ADDIE. [*Smugly.*] To entertain myself. I've always been my own best company, Mr. Bishop.

PAUL. [*Quizzically.*] Well—that makes it nice.

ADDIE. Well—Mr. Bishop—this morning I—I don't know how I could have done such an awful thing—but I blurted out to Papa that I went frequently to the bank—and when he asked me why I went there—I—I— Oh, Mr. Bishop, this is awful—I told him I went in there to see you.

PAUL. Me? [*As* ADDIE *nods and smiles—his interest and amusement grow.*] Say, what d'you know about that—a fan!

ADDIE. [*Fearful he's laughing at her—starts to flounder.*] Well, I wanted to sound reasonable and—and you're the best-looking one in the bank and—

PAUL. [*His amusement on the increase, nevertheless reveals a touch of male vanity.*] Now, wait a minute.

ADDIE. [*Still fearful he's laughing at her, crisps up.*] You wouldn't have to be Adonis to be that, Mr. Bishop.

PAUL. [*Still laughing.*] You've got no argument there, Miss Bemis.

ADDIE. [*Further resenting his levity, grows taut.*] It's nothing to laugh about, Mr. Bishop. My father's a—very peculiar man. And sometimes when he gets violent— [*Wincing, she "unconsciously" feels her bandaged wrist.*]

PAUL. Did he do that?

ADDIE. Yes!

PAUL. Say, that's terrible. Let me see it. [*She pulls back bandage reluctantly.*] Where is it?

ADDIE. There!

PAUL. Oh!

ADDIE. [*With super dramatics.*] Well—it hurts like fury!

PAUL. I see.

[ADDIE *feels that she's put him properly in his place and relaxes a trace.*]

ADDIE. [*Revelling in her situation.*] I had no idea Papa'd ever get so violent about—about— [*Taking a desperate grip on herself.*] Well, men don't interest me, Mr. Bishop, they never have. I mean everyone's always taken it for granted that I have my work, and the subject's never even come up! But today, Papa can't seem to drop it. He gets worse and worse. And a little while ago he called up and told me—well, he told me he was going to "find you and spoil your good looks," Mr. Bishop, "for life."

PAUL. But where does the old boy get these fantastic ideas?

ADDIE. [*After a moment's hesitation.*] They come in bottles.

PAUL. I see! But to want to beat a fellow up, even if you did come to the bank on my account.

ADDIE. Oh! You don't think I did come on your account?

PAUL. Why no! I wish you had.

ADDIE. You do?

PAUL. [*Caught.*] Uh! Uh—

ADDIE. [*Deflated.*] Oh! You're just being polite the way you are to everyone at the bank.

PAUL. Well—well I—

ADDIE. Well, anyway if I'd known what sort of places you spend your time in, Mr. Bishop, I might have chosen another bank.

PAUL. You mean this place? [*She nods, he smiles.*] What's wrong with it?

ADDIE. —Wrong with it? [*As she looks about, an overpowering distaste for the place and for everybody in it bursts through all her pretenses and gives us a hint of fanatical intolerance.*] I suppose it's all right, if you're satisfied to mix with scum.

PAUL. [*Amazed at her vehemence.*] Scum?

ADDIE. [*Eyes glittering with a bitter self-righteousness.*] I've never been in here before, but I know what goes on. We've got a roomer who works here. I find things out. I ask him.

PAUL. [*Still amazed.*] "What goes on"? Well—"what"—for instance?

ADDIE. Fights—and assignations! Things that law-abiding people report to the Police.

PAUL. The Police? Oh, now, Miss Bemis!

[ADDIE *reacts, biting her lip. Having started out to charm and interest* PAUL, *she has put her foot in it.* GAIL *goes back to the bar.*]

ADDIE. [*Trying to undo her faux-pas.*] I—I'm sorry. I'm afraid I was born with ideals that are a little bit too high.

PAUL. [*The subject of ideals suddenly dissipating his in-*

terest.] I see! [*Rises.*] Well, Miss Bemis, it's nice to have met you.

ADDIE. [*Intent on his not getting away. Rises.*] But what about my father?

PAUL. [*Impatiently.*] Well? What about him?

ADDIE. Well—I just wanted to warn you, Mr. Bishop—that's all. You see I—I've grown to respect you, Mr. Bishop, going to the bank and all and I—uh—

PAUL. Yes?

ADDIE. And—I—I wouldn't want anything to happen to you because of me—I mean I wouldn't want any harm to come to you, not for anything in the world.

PAUL. Well, that's very nice of you, Miss Bemis. Now you just forget all about it and run along! Good night.

ADDIE. [*Wanly.*] Good night. [*He starts to return to* MAUDE. *Frantic at losing* PAUL, ADDIE *calls after him.*] Oh, Mr. Bishop! [*He stops and turns. He goes to her.*] I hope you don't think I was alluding to you, when I used that—that term.

PAUL. [*Beginning to be a trace impatient with her.*] What term?

ADDIE. [*Blushing.*] —Scum.

PAUL. [*Genially.*] Oh, don't you worry! I've been called worse than that. [*Again he starts to go.*]

ADDIE. [*In a sudden outburst.*] Oh, dear! [PAUL *turns again.*] Or Miss Carson either. Oh—I ought to have my mouth washed out with soap. Please forgive me.

PAUL. [*Quizzically.*] Will you stop your worrying and relax?

ADDIE. I'll try.

PAUL. Well goodbye, Miss Bemis. And I promise next time you come to the bank I'll recognize you.

ADDIE. [*This degrading compliment is the most unkind of all.* ADDIE *now knows her whole venture after* PAUL *has come to nothing.*] Goodbye, Mr. Bishop.

[PAUL *crosses to* MAUDE *and* ADDIE *goes back to her table, starts to put on her galoshes, looks over toward* MAUDE *and getting fresh inspiration proceeds toward their table. During this* MAUDE *is questioning* PAUL.] ·

MAUDE. What did she want?

PAUL. Just business, Honey.

MAUDE. I should think you'd be able to get your business done at the bank. Come on finish your drink.

ADDIE. [*Right of table.*] I forgot to say goodbye to you, Miss Carson.

MAUDE. [*Looks up, sees her.*] Oh! Goodbye.

[ADDIE, *however, does not go but remains looking at* MAUDE *as if in a trance.* MAUDE, *studying her expression, reacts with curiosity.*]

ADDIE. [*Snapping to.*] Oh! I was wondering about your hair.

MAUDE. My hair?

ADDIE. Yes. How you get it to stay so—so exquisite in this weather?

MAUDE. [*Beginning to be a little flattered.*] Why it's just in the know-how, that's all.

ADDIE. I wish you'd tell me something I could do with mine.

MAUDE. [*Begins to look her over.*] —Well—let's see it.

[ADDIE *takes off hat and leans toward her, looking longingly at the chair.*] Yes, your hair's pretty—uh—fine. Perhaps if you'd— [*Unthinkingly.*] Sit down. [ADDIE *sits quickly, Right of table.*] You ought to brush it more—at least a hundred strokes—every morning.

ADDIE. Do you think I could ever wear it like you do yours?

MAUDE. [*Takes a long look at her. Then—*] No, I wouldn't try that.

[*At which point* DAD *comes up with the drinks—serves* MAUDE—*then* PAUL—*stands Right of* PAUL.]

ADDIE. Oh, you're having some drinks.

PAUL. [*Cornered.*] Why yes! Won't you join us?

ADDIE. [*Moving in closer to the table.*] Oh no, thanks. I'll just sit.

PAUL. [*Impatient over her stalling.*] Go ahead and have something! It'll iron out all those troubles you've got and make you feel fine.

ADDIE. Oh, no, thanks. [*With a touch of sweet smugness.*] I'm "on the water wagon." [*She laughs.*]

PAUL. Some ginger ale, then.

ADDIE. [*As if embarrassed at so much attention, gives in.*] Oh, all right, since you insist, thank you.

PAUL. [*To* DAD.] Make it a Horse's Neck.

ADDIE. [*Suspicious.*] You said ginger ale!

MAUDE. That's all it is, Mrs. Bemis, with some lemon peel!

ADDIE. I'm "Miss" Bemis.

MAUDE. [*Beginning to be thoroughly fed up.*] I'm sorry!

ADDIE. [*Turning to* DAD.] I thought it was a "drink," Mr. Malone.

DAD. [*As he leaves—crossing to bar.*] Well—bless your heart!

[*During this interchange with* DAD, MAUDE *and* PAUL *engage in pantomime over being "stuck" with* ADDIE. *She finally turns, catches them in it and they quickly straighten out.*]

PAUL. [*In order to be alone with* MAUDE *and square himself.*] What d'you say we have some more music, Miss Bemis?

ADDIE. That would be—lovely.

PAUL. Suppose you pick it out yourself. Want to? [*He hands* ADDIE *a nickel.*]

ADDIE. Pick it out?

PAUL. Yes, on the juke box.

ADDIE. Oh—dear. [*Rises, crosses up Left Center, then turns to* MAUDE.] Is there any special tune you'd like to hear, Miss Carson?

MAUDE. It doesn't matter. Anything but "Melancholy Baby." It makes me melancholy and I've a headache. [*Self-consciously,* ADDIE *goes to the juke box where, with elaborate care, she proceeds to make a selection. With sarcasm.*] Well, Paulie! I thought I had a date with you?

PAUL. I like that! Who asked her to sit down?

MAUDE. Well, I didn't mean all night.

PAUL. [*Entranced with her beauty.*] Let's have this drink and go home.

MAUDE. [*Shocked.*] To your place?

PAUL. Why not?

MAUDE. You know very well why not. You promised to wait.

PAUL. [*Suddenly ashamed.*] I'm sorry, Honey. [*Kisses her hand.*] That better?

[MAUDE *wrinkles her nose and nods.* ADDIE *succeeds in starting the juke box on the same record to which* MAUDE *objected. She turns to* MAUDE *as if in abject apology.*]

ADDIE. [*Crossing down Center.*] Oh! I thought I changed that record.

MAUDE. It's all right.

ADDIE. [*Returns to table and sits.*] I'm so sorry! And you with a headache.

MAUDE. Oh, never mind!

[DAD *brings Horse's Neck to table.*]

PAUL. [*Indicating Horse's Neck.*] Won't you drink to us, Miss Bemis? [*Arm around* MAUDE.] On the Fourth of July we're being married.

ADDIE. [*A little too brightly.*] Oh, how lovely!

[*As* ADDIE *picks up the glass, she subconsciously reveals her shock by letting it slip through her fingers, splattering herself with its contents.*]

MAUDE. [*Her alarm over so minor an accident revealing an excessive canniness.* ADDIE *and* PAUL *rise.*] You've spilled that on my dress!

[DAD *comes down with cloth.*]

ADDIE. I'll pay for cleaning it, Miss Carson!

PAUL. Why, it never touched you, dear! She's the one who got it. [*Taking out his handkerchief, turns to* ADDIE.] If you'll allow me, Miss Bemis— [*As he takes her arm to dab at the wet spot, a thrill suddenly shoots through* ADDIE, *so violent as to cause a little gasp. Unconscious of her emotions, he dabs away.*] Hope you don't mind me holding hands with you.

ADDIE. [*Gulps—then—a strange, dazed look coming into her face.*] —Mind? Oh, no.

[DAD, *moving into scene with a bar rag. He starts to mop up table.* ADDIE *sits.*]

PAUL. It's just what we deserved, anyway, having you drink our health in that stuff. [*Sits. To* DAD.] Bring her a Pink Lady.

DAD. [*To* ADDIE, *expecting her to countermand the order.*] —Addie?

[*She hesitates.*]

PAUL. [*Arm around* MAUDE.] We're being married! Isn't that reason enough to go off the wagon?

ADDIE. [*In sudden desperation turns to* DAD.] Bring me a Pink Lady.

DAD. That drink has liquor in it, Addie darlin'.

ADDIE. Bring me a Pink Lady!

DAD. [*After a hesitation.*] —Okay. [*Shaking his head, he goes sadly for the drink.*]

PAUL. There!

MAUDE. [*As* PAUL *starts to put his handkerchief in his pocket.*] That handkerchief's wet, darling! Look out.

ADDIE. [*Quickly—taking handkerchief from* MAUDE.] I'll launder your handkerchief!

PAUL. [*With a little smile.*] Oh—that's not necessary!

ADDIE. I've got a washing machine. It's nothing. [*Confused, she tucks the handkerchief in her pocketbook.*]

MAUDE. Please stop being so upset, Miss Bemis. [ADDIE'S *reply is a sickly grin and* MAUDE *now turns to* PAUL.] Did you get the blueprints back from the building company, dear?

PAUL. Sorry, darling. I didn't have a single moment all day. [*Turning to* ADDIE, *speaks with interest and pride.*] We've got a little place nearly built out on Sheridan Avenue, Roselle.

ADDIE. Oh! Right on Warinanco Park!

PAUL. Do you know that neighborhood?

ADDIE. [*Still dazed.*] Oh, yes! It's beautiful.

PAUL. We think it's nice.

MAUDE. [*Preoccupied with something.*] Paulie! Let me have your pen.

[*He gives it to her.*]

PAUL. [*He goes on warmly, playing with his cigarette as he talks, exuding a sensuous and loving satisfaction in his day dream and not noting that* MAUDE *is starting to draw something in the magazine.* ADDIE *divides her attention between him and* MAUDE, *studying them narrowly.*] Of course the little place is nothing fancy—sort of Early American—you know what I mean. [*Arm around* MAUDE.]
ADDIE. Yes, I know.

PAUL. It's got a small yard—but it's got a barbecue in it—

I'm pretty good at steaks, so days we invite company, if she isn't in the mood for cooking—well—I'm pretty good. [*During the above,* DAD *puts the Pink Lady on the table.* PAUL *continues his day dream.*] I've put myself a workshop in the basement too—I had one when I was a kid. [*Hands drink to* ADDIE.]

ADDIE. You did?

PAUL. The first thing I'm going to make is a dressing table for Maude.

ADDIE. Oh!

PAUL. And I'm going to fix a little ice-box in my den for beer. The fellows'll appreciate that and it will keep us out of Maude's hair the night we play poker. Won't it, Sweets?

MAUDE. [*Completely disinterested.*] Uh-huh.

PAUL. [*He sighs deeply in satisfaction, then, indicating* ADDIE'S *glass.*] Don't you want your drink, Miss Bemis?

ADDIE. [*Still dazed.*] Oh! Oh, yes.

PAUL. It'll be all ready when we get back from our honeymoon. So, you see, it's a pure set-up for happiness. Go ahead.

ADDIE. [*In dazed contemplation of* MAUDE.] Well—here's to the pure set-up for happiness. [*Expecting to gag on her first drink,* ADDIE *gingerly takes a sip and reacts pleasantly surprised—then takes a second sip.*]

PAUL. [*Indicating drink.*] Is it all right?

ADDIE. I don't know. I never had one before.

MAUDE. [*Incredulous.*] Never had a Pink Lady?

[ADDIE *shakes her head.*]

PAUL. [*With real interest.*] How long have you been on the wagon, Miss Bemis?

ADDIE. Always.

PAUL. What?

ADDIE. Always.

[*A pause—then—*]

MAUDE. Well! That's a good way to stay sober, isn't it?— [ADDIE *shoots her a look, then, as if subtly prompted by this dumb remark, takes another sip.*] You haven't asked why I want the blueprints back, Paulie.

PAUL. Why, honey?

MAUDE. This morning I got the most practical idea out of this "Good Housekeeping Magazine."

PAUL. Again?

MAUDE. Yes. I want to find out whether we could run some water pipes from the kitchen through to your den so it could be turned into an extra bedroom and bath, just in case we ever want to sell.

PAUL. There goes my den, Miss Bemis. [*To* MAUDE.] But, Honey, why think of selling before the joint's even finished?

MAUDE. [*Cutely insistent.*] Paulie! Do I get the blueprints?

PAUL. [*With sardonic resignation.*] Well—what do you think?

MAUDE. Oh, darling, thanky!. Thanky two times. [*She rubs her nose against* PAUL'S.]

[*At which point* ADDIE *drains her liquor to the dregs.*]

PAUL. Cute, isn't she?

ADDIE. [*Nods, then looks off toward* DAD *almost as a cry for help.*] Mr. Malone!

DAD. [*As he approaches.*] What is it, Addie?

ADDIE. [*Almost with desperation.*] I want to buy some drinks! [*Turning to* MAUDE.] Will you have another Pink Lady, Miss Carson?

MAUDE. [*With maidenly restraint.*] Oh, nothing more, thanks.

ADDIE. [*Turning to* PAUL.] —Mr. Bishop?

PAUL. Why, yes. I'll have another Old-fashioned.

DAD. [*Starts away.*] Yes, sir.

ADDIE. [*Rising, calls after him.*] And the same for me that I had just now! [*Sits.*]

DAD. —Oh, no, Addie!

ADDIE. Another Pink Lady, Mr. Malone.

DAD. [*Sadly, after hesitation.*] Very well.

[ADDIE *subsides.*]

MAUDE. [*Secure in her captivity of* PAUL, *starts to launch into another little project.*] Guess where we're going on our honeymoon, Miss Bemis?

ADDIE. Where?

MAUDE. To the golden state of—California. Just think of it. A whole honeymoon right in that California sunshine!

ADDIE. You don't think all that sunshine will make it seem a little—public?

PAUL. [*Beginning to thoroughly enjoy* ADDIE's *ribaldry.*] I see what you mean, Miss Bemis.

MAUDE. —Paulie! Perhaps those movies will want me to have a screen test while we're out there.

PAUL. They're all blind, Honey, if they don't.

MAUDE. Thanky, dear. Paulie, we might like Hollywood so much we'll want to stay there.

PAUL. [*Alarmed.*] —Stay there?

MAUDE. [*Wheedlingly.*] —For a little while, Paulie.

PAUL. [*Gravely.*] I'd like to know how we'd get the money for that, Sweets?

MAUDE. [*Deciding she's gone far enough.*] Well—let's not worry about that now!

ADDIE. Why should you? With that extra bedroom and bath you can sell the house— [*Snaps her fingers.*] Just like that!

PAUL. [*To* MAUDE—*with increasing gravity.*] Say, Honey, is that your idea?

MAUDE. [*Confused and stammering.*] Why—why—of course not, Paulie. But after we got out to Hollywood—if you just happened to like it—and we decided not to come back—and—

ADDIE. [*Cutting in—to* MAUDE.] He could get a job in a bank out there, couldn't he?

MAUDE. [*Warming up.*] Of course!

PAUL. But, Honey! I haven't got any connections out there.

ADDIE. Don't worry! She'll meet a lot of nice men. [*Turning to* MAUDE.] Maybe he won't even have to work, will he?

MAUDE. Maybe not!

PAUL. [*Suddenly realizing where the conversation has taken them.*] Well, holy smoke, Maude! There's a few things we've got to get straightened out.

[*At which point* DAD *comes to* MAUDE'S *rescue by stepping up with the drinks.*]

ADDIE. [*Ironically.*] Let's hope this drink can iron out all your troubles, Mr. Bishop. [*She pays* DAD *and proceeds to drink.*]

[MAUDE, *in deep distress, gestures to* PAUL *to get rid of* ADDIE, *at which point two gay old girls in their sixties blow in exuberantly from the street. They are known as* TOT *and* EMMA.]

GAIL. [*Going to greet them.*] Hello, Tot dear! How're you, Emma?

TOT. [*Moving below door.*] Hello, Gail! What a night.

EMMA. [*Crossing to table No. 3.*] Fine weather for ducks, eh, Honey?

GAIL. Where've you girls been in all this rain?

TOT. To the Bijou, darlin'. Some show!

EMMA. Yeah. It was Jane Russell. They ought to give that girl two Oscars for what we saw tonight.

GAIL. No foolin'.

TOT. [*Crossing Center.*] It was intensely dramatic. The first time she met this civil engineer they thought they hated each other.

EMMA. That was before the rainstorm. You see she was forced to take refuge in his hunting lodge.

TOT. Then came the scene that intrigued me, in front of the fireplace. Her sweater had shrunk in the rain—and it suddenly hit him that he had loved her all along.

EMMA. Then he chased her around the room a little.

TOT. And they wound up in a lovely grapple on a bearskin rug. [*Crossing back to* EMMA.]

[*They* BOTH *sit at table No. 3.*]

MAUDE. Really! That kind of talk is quite uncalled for.

PAUL. Oh, take it easy.

ADDIE. I know how Miss Carson feels. She approves of sex but thinks it should be dainty.

MAUDE. Paul! [*Rises.*]

PAUL. Sit down, Honey! She's got you to a T.

[DON *puts two nickels in juke box and "Honeysuckle Rose" plays first.*]

MAUDE. Paulie! If you don't get rid of— [*Sits.*]

[DON *and* JUNE *and* BELLA *and* GABE *start dancing.*]

PAUL. Sit down, Sweets. [*He rises and goes to* GAIL.] Gail! Do you suppose your two friends could look after that Bemis girl till she decides to go home?

GAIL. D'you mean Tot and Emma?

PAUL. Yes. If I should dance her over to their table.

GAIL. Why, sure.

PAUL. Explain it to Maude.

GAIL. Okay, Honey.

PAUL. [*Crosses to* ADDIE.] Would you do me the honor to dance with me?

ADDIE. [*The Pink Lady halfway to her lips, looks up at him.*

Incredulous.] Would you do me the honor to repeat that please?

PAUL. I said I'd like to dance.

ADDIE. [*Skeptically looking at him through slit eyelids, sure that he intends to make fun of her again.*] With me?

PAUL. Why not?

ADDIE. —Why—not! [*As* ADDIE *studies him a moment in silence, a giddy feeling begins to come over her that maybe she was wrong about* PAUL'S *mockery. Perhaps she is an attractive human being. She takes time to toss off the last of her drink and rises. Followed by the vastly relieved gaze of* MAUDE, PAUL *escorts* ADDIE *to the dance floor. He takes her in his arms and for a moment they dance silently. Finally, as if this is all too blissful for belief,* ADDIE *looks up at him. Wanting desperately to know his attitude.*] Why did you ask me to dance, Mr. Bishop?

PAUL. [*Politely.*] Because I wanted to.

ADDIE. What made you—want to?

PAUL. [*A little bit stumped.*] Because you're—an intelligent young lady.

ADDIE. [*Now sufficiently assured to fish for further compliments.*] Do you always want to dance with intelligent young ladies?

PAUL. [*Grinning.*] Never danced with one in my whole life!

ADDIE. [*Her heart leaping.*] Thank you! [*A moment's silence—then—in sudden confession.*] D'you know something? I always have the impression folks don't like me.

PAUL. Do you, now?

ADDIE. I try not to show it and I work very hard to be pleasant to everybody—but that's the impression I have.

PAUL. [*Heartily.*] Well, you just snap out of it!

ADDIE. [*Exultantly.*] That's what I'm doing! Snapping right out of it! [*She starts dancing with a little added style.*]

PAUL. [*A trace surprised at her gracefulness.*] You dance very well, Miss Bemis.

ADDIE. If I do, it's thanks to the Cosmopolitan dance course.

[*Taking off jacket and leaving it on her chair at table No. 2.*]

PAUL. Oh—you went to dancing school?

ADDIE. [*Smugly.*] No. Dancing school came to me.

PAUL. [*Amazed and curious.*] By—mail?

ADDIE. Complete in twelve lessons—with diagrams. Mother subscribed to it just before she—passed away.

PAUL. [*Touched.*] Oh!

ADDIE. She said she hoped it would bring me pleasure as long as I lived. But she'd be tickled pink if she could see me now.

[*Overcome by barroom emotion which, like all such feeling, has a very real basis, she buries her face in his breast, making PAUL pretty uncomfortable.*

During the above MANUEL and MARGOT, the song and dance team enter. They are South Americans, the man in rather shabby white tie and tails—the girl in a none-too-fresh dance creation which is partly covered by a raincoat. They are obviously lovers and seem to be cheerful, happy-go-lucky types, not in the least bogged down by their jobless situa-

tion. Trailing them is their accompanist, BERT, *a typical night club character.*]

GAIL. [*Going Right to greet them.*) Well—hello, kids!

MANUEL. How are you, lovely lady? [*He proceeds to kiss her hand.*]

[*"Honeysuckle Rose" stops.*]

MARGOT. [*During the above.*] Good evening, Gail. [*Indicating* BERT.] This is our accompanist, Bert.

GAIL. It's a pleasure, Bert. Too bad I haven't got a few more customers for your tryout but— [*Juke box record of "I Haven't Got a Worry in the World" starts. The three couples start dancing again. At which point she breaks off, her attention taken by a surly, drunken figure who staggers in from the street and stands weaving about in the glass enclosure trying to close the outside door. It is* BEMIS. *In alarm, speaking to* DAD, *who is at bar.*] Oh, Dad!

DAD. [*To* HERMAN *as he sees* BEMIS.] Good God, it's Bemis.

[*Tosses a quick worried glance at* ADDIE *as he starts for door.*]

GAIL. [*To* DAD.] Tell him there's a cop in here—looking for him.

DAD. [*As he hurries into glass enclosure.*] I hope it works!

[*During the following dialogue* DAD *stops* BEMIS *in the enclosure, and standing in front of him to prevent his seeing* ADDIE, *puts up an argument for* BEMIS *to leave.*]

GAIL. [*Addressing the trio of entertainers, her gaze on* BEMIS.] That drunk's got me worried.

MANUEL. Drunk is right! He was talking to us out there.

MARGOT. [*Piping up with a shudder.*] He says he's going to kill somebody!

GAIL. [*With enforced casualness, her gaze never leaving* BEMIS.] That so?

MANUEL. Yeah. Some guy that works in a bank is trying to steal his daughter.

GAIL. Steal *her?*

[GAIL *tosses an incredulous glance at* ADDIE *and the reluctant* PAUL, *during which* DAD *succeeds in ushering* BEMIS *out into the street.*]

MARGOT. Look, Gail! He's gone.

GAIL. Yeah. [*They all watch* DAD *a moment as he looks out after* BEMIS *to make sure he's on his way. Then, as* DAD, *apparently convinced, closes the door, all react in relief and* GAIL *turns to the trio.*] Sit down and take it easy, kids.

MARGOT, MANUEL *and* BERT. [*In unison, as they start for table No. 5 up Center.*] Thanks, Gail. Thanks a million.

GAIL. [*Turning to* DAD *as he comes from glass enclosure.*] What about Bemis?

DAD. He's gone down to Al's place.

GAIL. [*A big sigh of relief.*] Good!

DAD. If he makes trouble there, Al might slip him a mickey.

GAIL. —Yeah! Well—it's coming to him.

ADDIE. Don't you just love that song, Mr. Bishop?

PAUL. Yes. It's my favorite.

ADDIE. How odd! Why it's mine, too.

[*At which point* DON *has grabbed the mike and bringing down near the dance floor starts to croon the words.*]

DON.

> "My heart is in a flurry
> My pulse is in a hurry
> But I haven't got a Bluebird—"

ADDIE. [*Interrupting to correct him.*] "Worry." "—haven't—got—a—worry—in—the—world."

DON. [*Tries to follow her but realizing she knows the words drags her to the mike to sing.*] All right. You know the words so you sing it.

ADDIE. [*Struggling against him.*] What! Oh, no.

PAUL. Go on! I'd like to hear it.

ADDIE. Really? [*She starts to sing nervously but finally gains confidence and to the great amusement of* ALL *finishes the chorus like a blues singer. The music swells into the last half of the chorus and she and* PAUL *finish their dance with great flourish.*]

PAUL. [*Trying to cover his relief.*] That was—swell. And now I'd like you to meet—

[*He takes her arm to lead her to* TOT *and* EMMA *but* ADDIE *refuses to budge.*]

ADDIE. [*Desperately launching a conversation, crossing down Right.*] How do you feel about your work, Mr. Bishop?

PAUL. [*A trace nonplussed.*] Me?

ADDIE. Yes! Do you love it—or—

[BERT *goes to piano and starts playing "When I Come Back."*]

PAUL. [*Interested, as always, in his work.*] Sure I love it! It's okay. And before the war it was swell, because I was younger then and not so—settled. But, gee, after a fellow comes out of the Army, he sort of feels he's due for a promotion.

ADDIE. From what I hear, a fellow sort of felt that way when he was in the Army.

PAUL. [*Intrigued by her comment, laughs.*] Yes—that's right. [*During the above, the record has run out. Studying* ADDIE.] Say—where do you find out all these things?

ADDIE. I listen. A lot of men in uniform went past my desk at the place I work.

PAUL. I see. [*Again he starts to lead her to* TOT *and* EMMA.] And now I'd like—

ADDIE. [*Again stopping him.*] Where did you meet Miss Carson?

PAUL. [*Perfectly matter-of-fact.*] At a bar. That's where you meet girls.

ADDIE. Oh! Of course! Now I'm glad I came to one.

PAUL. [*Evasively.*] Sure. And now—

[*Again he starts to lead her from the dance floor, but* ADDIE *holds back.*]

ADDIE. [*They start dancing again.*] But even if I hadn't, we'd have gotten together some place. You see, "The Gods are to each other not unknown." [*Quizzical over such high-flown language,* PAUL *gives her a look.*] That's from Emerson—Philosophy—aisle nine—under the steel engraving of George Washington.

PAUL. Oh! At the library, eh?

ADDIE. That's where I work. [*With kidding accusation.*] And where you never come.

PAUL. [*With just a trace of interest.*] I used to like to read. When I was nine years old I could recite "The Shooting of Dan McGrew" without a stop. And I knew all the parts of the Bible that—you know—kids aren't supposed to look at. [*Boyishly.*] My old man gave me five dollars once for learning the books of the Bible. Want to hear me say off the minor prophets?

ADDIE. Sure!

PAUL. [*Speaking in one breath.*] Hosea, Joel, Amos, Obadiah, Jonah, Micah, Nahum, Habakkuk, Zephaniah, Haggai, Zechariah, Malachi. What d'you think of that?

[*The piano music stops.*]

ADDIE. It's wonderful!

PAUL. [*A trace wistfully.*] I used to be able to say them much faster. I ought to read more. I like it. But when I come out of that bank I'm so tired—

ADDIE. [*Eagerly—quickly.*] You should have somebody read to you!

PAUL. [*Amused.*] Do you mean—Maudie? [PAUL *looks to* MAUDE.]

ADDIE. Yes—or somebody! [*Suddenly calling to* BERT.] Oh, Mr. Music Man. [BERT *looks toward her.*] "I Haven't Got a Worry in the World." [*Nodding,* BERT *segues into it.*] *To* PAUL.] Oh, wonderful! We're going to have an encore.

PAUL. [*Tosses a glance at* MAUDE, *who sits glowering—then —fairly hustling* ADDIE *off the dance floor to* TOT *and* EMMA'S *table No. 3.*] D'you mind, Miss Bemis—I'd like to have you meet some old friends of mine. Good evening, ladies!

TOT and EMMA. [*Having been primed by* GAIL.] Good evening, Pal. Nice to see you.

PAUL. This is a little friend of mine—Miss Bemis. .

TOT. Glad to know you, dear.

EMMA. Sit down and cut up a few touches with us, won't you, Honey?

ADDIE. I'd love to, but Mr. Bishop and I—we're dancing.

PAUL. [*Pulling out chair for her.*] Maybe you'd better visit awhile with the ladies, Miss Bemis. [*With a glance toward* MAUDE.] You see how it is—I have a little problem of—jealousy to deal with.

ADDIE. [*Wanting to hear the thrilling words again.*] Would you mind repeating that, please?

PAUL. Miss Carson—she's probably a little jealous.

ADDIE. [*Reverting to her super-humility.*] Oh, but *I* haven't got anything that she has!

PAUL. You haven't got anything to worry about. You're all right.

ADDIE. [*Her heart leaping.*] Thanks. [*She sinks into the proffered chair Left of table No. 3.*]

PAUL. [*To* TOT *and* EMMA.] I think Miss Bemis might like some black coffee. [*As he beckons for* DAD.] And I wish you'd have a little something too, on me.

[BERT *segues into "I Don't Know Why."*]

TOT. [*To* EMMA.] Ain't he the sweetheart, now? [*Turning to* PAUL.] Thanks, Mr. Pope.

PAUL. You're promoting me. The name's Bishop. [*He leaves them, goes to* MAUDE *and they start dancing down Left.*]

ADDIE. [*With drunken suspicion, turns to* EMMA *and* TOT.] I thought he said you were old friends!

EMMA. [*Gaily.*] What he meant, dearie, was *old* friends.

ADDIE. [*Suspicious.*] Where'd he meet you?

EMMA. Oh—we get around.

TOT. Emma works in millinery—the Elite One-Price Hat Shoppe. And I take in roomers.

EMMA. [*In order to give* TOT *a good mark.*] Roomers without special privileges, you understand.

TOT. [*Regretfully and nostalgically.*] Yes, Honey! This new city administration's like a strait-jacket. It's taking all of the charm out of Newark.

EMMA. But we have our dreams! [*She sighs.*]

ADDIE. [*Brooding.*] —He only asked me to dance to get me over here!

TOT. [*Always spoiling for a fight.*] Well, why don't you have it out with him?

ADDIE. [*With drunken dignity.*] Oh—I wouldn't want to make a scene.

TOT. Why not?

EMMA. That's right, dear! There's nothing like a good old-fashioned lovers' brawl!

ADDIE. [*Indignant.*] Lovers? We're not—lovers.

EMMA. Listen, dear—if you don't like it don't knock it.

DAD. [*Stepping up.*] Well, ladies!

EMMA. Make mine a double Scotch.

TOT. A double Bourbon, with beer as an escort. [*To* ADDIE.] What is it for you, dear—black coffee?

ADDIE. [*Beginning to sizzle over* PAUL.] A double Pink Lady.

DAD. [*With a gasp.*] Oh, no, Addie!

ADDIE. [*Pugnaciously.*] A double Pink Lady, Mr. Malone!

TOT. But that's a tart's drink, Honey.

ADDIE. [*Looks at* TOT *a moment, stunned.*] —It is? [*Her gaze, as if in sudden revelation, goes to pick up* MAUDE.]

EMMA. [*To* DAD.] Go get her a little straight Scotch, Junior. Those mixed drinks is too decadent. [*She pronounces it decayed-ent.*]

DAD. You don't want it, Addie, do you?

ADDIE. [*Her thoughtful gaze still on* MAUDE.] —Yes!

DAD. Straight Scotch? Oh, Addie—where's your dignity?

ADDIE. Maybe we Scotch invented it because we couldn't stand our dignity.

[DAD *goes sadly to bar.*]

TOT. Good for you, dear! That was telling him.

ADDIE. It's just a gag.

EMMA. Him and his narrow-mindedness! He ought to get a job in a dairy lunch.

ADDIE. [*Her thoughtful gaze returns once more to* MAUDE.] —So, it's a tart's drink, is it?

TOT. That's right, darlin'—generally ordered to impress a chump. I've toyed with many a one in my day. Heigh-ho!

[*Piano music stops and* BERT *returns to his table.* MAUDE *and* PAUL *sit at their table.*]

ADDIE. That's just what he is!

TOT. Who's what?

ADDIE. That word you said. That's what he is! [*Her gaze on* MAUDE.] And that other word you said—that's what she is!

EMMA. Yeah! Now you bring the subject up, it sticks out all over her, the jerk.

TOT. It sure does! She wouldn't fool anybody but a man.

EMMA. Well—who else do you need to fool?

DAD. [*Steps up with drinks.*] Here you are, ladies.

TOT. And high time too! [*Picking up glass, calls across to* PAUL.] Sst! Mr. Pope! [PAUL *looks up, raises a glass.*] Here's thanks for the beverage.

[PAUL *smiles and nods.*]

EMMA. Here's to you!

ADDIE. [*Defiant speaks across to* PAUL.] And here's—against you! [*In supreme derision.*] —Married. Huh!

EMMA. Married? [*In surprise.*] Do you mean that clambake is "legalized"?

ADDIE. It will be the Fourth of July—Independence Day— what a mockery!

TOT. Look, dear. If you're half the woman I think you are, you'll tip the poor guy off.

EMMA. That's the idea! Drag it all out into the open. Raise a stink. You know—finesse.

ADDIE. Finesse?

TOT. Sure! Make him realize two months after they're married she'll be giving him the finger.

ADDIE. [*All at sea.*] Giving him the—? [TOT *nods and illustrates with the well-known gesture.*] Do you mean another man? [TOT *nods.*] I think she's giving it to him now!

EMMA. Anybody we know?

ADDIE. D'you know any—Italians?

EMMA. [*Giving it due consideration.*] Uhm— Not at the moment. [*Leans back.*]

TOT. What sort of Italians, dear?

ADDIE. The boss she works for—at a Beauty Shoppe.

TOT. Oh! The type that mixes business with the business.

EMMA. Say, why don't you get the guy down here, and have the whole thing out?

TOT. Sure! A rainy night's the ideal time to stir things up.

EMMA. It's a night like this that anything can happen!

TOT. You owe it to yourself, dear.

ADDIE. If I knew where he was—I'd do it.

TOT. Couldn't you get him on the phone? [*She pronounces it* "Foam."]

ADDIE. [*After a moment's deep thought.*] —I've forgotten his name.

EMMA. Italian. Let's see. Is it Luigi? [ADDIE *shakes her*

head.] Schiaperelli? [ADDIE *shakes her head again.*] Gustafson? No! That's Spanish.

TOT. Try and think, darling.

EMMA. Think hard. You owe it to yourself. Once you get him down here things'll start to pop. The fat'll be in the fire. The joint'll start in jumpin'.

ADDIE. The joint'll start in jumpin'?

TOT. Sure. It'll be amateur night in a monkey house.

ADDIE. But I can't think of his name. I'm a failure. I've let you down.

TOT. Look at the poor kid. She's heartachy.

EMMA. We know just how you feel, dear. Tot and me both loved in our time.

TOT. And madly.

EMMA. Look, Honey, don't die on us. [*Calls off to* DAD.] Oh, Junior!

TOT. Here! Perk up, Honey, and try a little of my lipstick. You're more than welcome. It's Man Trap Red.

DAD. What'll it be, ladies?

EMMA. These are on me, girls. What'll you have?

[*Music starts.*]

TOT. [*To* DAD.] The same.

EMMA. The same for me.[*To* ADDIE.] And you, dear?

ADDIE. [*Listening.*] That's pretty!

EMMA. What's pretty?

ADDIE. That music—

TOT. [*To* EMMA.] She's hearing things!

EMMA. What'll you have to drink, dear?

ADDIE. [*Giving the matter deep thought.*] Let's—see—I'll have— [*As she looks off at the bottles on the bar, one of them slowly begins to light up with a ruby glow.*] What's that bottle there?

TOT. Which one, dear?

ADDIE. That one! [*At which point the lighted bottle blinks and there emerges from it a lovely, musical sound.*] The one that's burbling at me— Don't you hear it?

TOT. Burbling?

DAD. Addie!

ADDIE. Yes—don't you hear it? That red one.

EMMA. She must mean the Sloe Gin, Tot.

TOT. Get her a good big dram of it, Dad. Go on, hurry.

[DAD *goes sadly to the bar while* HERMAN *picks up the bottle which still glows.*]

ADDIE. Funny! I didn't know drinks lit up!

EMMA. —Lit up, dear?

ADDIE. It's shining—just like a ruby! See it!

TOT. [*To* EMMA.] Now she's seeing things.

ADDIE. —Is it a tart's drink too?

EMMA. Sloe Gin? What would you say, Tottie?

TOT. Oh no—it's rather—uh—Oriental.

EMMA. It's more like a tonic.

TOT. And on top of Scotch it should prove most invigorating.

EMMA. You'll be a new girl, Honey, and you can use it.

MAUDE. [*At which point* MAUDE *laughs at something* PAUL *has said.*] Oh, Paulie.

ADDIE. [*A glance at* MAUDE *then bursting out.*] Nanino!

TOT. Nanino?

ADDIE. Nanino! That's the name.. The Italian's name.

EMMA. Tot! We've struck gold!

TOT. Go get him on the phone, dear. Hurry.

ADDIE. You mean now?

EMMA. Yes, now!

[DAD *brings drinks.*]

ADDIE. Thanks, Junior. [ADDIE *gulps drink, rises.*] Excuse me. I'm going to drag this all out in the open.

EMMA. You're a girl after my own heart, dolling.

TOT. Addie, we love you!

ADDIE. [*Starts away then turns back to them.*] You know what? You're my friends—the first friends I ever had in my whole life.

TOT. It's more than an honor, dear!

EMMA. And that goes for me likewise.

ADDIE. My first friends! [*She starts to phone.*] Oh, a nickel!

TOT. I think I've got one, Honey.

ADDIE. [*Starting toward bar.*] No, thanks, dear. I'll finance this thing myself. [*She passes* MAUDE *and picks up handbag from table.*] Pink Lady!

TOT. Emma, you started this.

EMMA. Yeah, but you egged her on.

TOT. Yeah, ain't it lovely. Anyhow the evening isn't going to be a klunk, after all.

ADDIE. [*With great dignity, handing* HERMAN *a dollar bill.*] Would you please give me some phone for the change, please. [HERMAN *takes the bill.* ADDIE *ponders her statement.*] Was there anything wrong what I just said?

HERMAN. I got you, lady.

[*He turns to cash register and as he punches it, instead of a click accompanying a "no sale" a delicate musical phrase sounds bring forth a sigh of bliss from* ADDIE.]

ADDIE. You play that beautifully.

HERMAN. [*Giving* ADDIE *the money.*] Here you are, lady.

ADDIE. Thank you. I'm going to drag this all out in the open.

[*She starts Right for phone in a jaunty step, circling to pick up her Sloe Gin from her table.*]

TOT. Rambunctious type of little bun she works up, doesn't she.

EMMA. Cute! Liquor gives her spirit.

DAD. Y-e-a-h! But if her Dad should happen to come in and catch her—drinking and all—it would just be murder. That's what! Murder.

TOT. And you wanted to go home after the movie!

ADDIE. [*Calling to* TOT *and* EMMA *as she dials.*] I've got it!

TOT. She's got it!

EMMA. We're off in a gallop.

ADDIE. [*Into phone.*] Hello! [*To* TOT *and* EMMA.] What did I say his name was?

TOT. Nanino.

ADDIE. [*Into phone.*] Hello. I want to speak to Mr. Nanino—

EMMA. Is he there?

ADDIE. He's coming— [*In phone. Belligerently.*] Hello, Mr. Nanino! Let's drag this all out in the open! You owe it to yourself. [*Turning to* TOT *and* EMMA.] He doesn't under-stand.

TOT. Be nice to him, dear!

EMMA. Sure, butter him up!

ADDIE. Mr. Nanino, dear! If you have any interest in a young lady whose name I cannot mention but whose initials are Maude Carson—it would be very much to your disadvantage to come over here— What?— Over here. [*Turning to* TOT *and* EMMA.] He wants to know where we are. Shall I tell him?

TOT *and* EMMA. Sure! Go ahead!

ADDIE. The Jersey Mecca Cocktail Bar. Good. I'm warning you, you'd better hurry. She's giving you her fingers—*her fingers.* [*She illustrates with gesture. Then listens.*] You'll find out something very much to your disadvantage. Good. [*She hangs up—then into phone without lifting receiver.*] Oh! Goodbye. [*Turning to* TOT *and* EMMA.] He's coming.

EMMA. Bully for you, dear.

TOT. Now, all you need is a drink!

ADDIE. All I need is—a drink! [*She picks up glass that she had left on telephone ledge and drains it. As she does so she notices the lily directly over the phone.*] Hello, Lily! [*The lily bursts slowly into full bloom in her face then quickly retracts. The warmth from the drinks cause her to open the scarf about her neck so that she appears to be in an extremely low-necked gown. As she now turns back to look at the people in the room she notices everybody swaying. She sits down Left of table No. 3. Then she rises and looks about again.* EVERYBODY *is still weaving. As the light effects begin to unfold and the music to swell she crosses to Center. Then in childish delight to* TOT *and* EMMA.] Look! The joint! It's jumping. Look! [*As she turns about with her arms triumphantly extended the music and effects reach an exciting climax and the Curtain falls.*]

END OF ACT ONE

ACT TWO

ACT TWO

SCENE: *As the Curtain rises slowly we hear the music pick up the same phrase on which it ended in Act One—but in a very low key. The stage is in darkness save for two spots of light. One is on* ADDIE, *who is in the same pose in which we last saw her. The other glows forth from a bottle of Creme de Menthe on the shelf beside the bar.*

By the time the Curtain has risen, a small but exciting voice rises from the glowing bottle. It says, "Yoo-hoo, Ad-die."

Now ADDIE *turns to focus on the bottle and, as she does, we note that her excitement and high spirits have made her look enticingly alive. Her color has heightened, her eyes are shining, her features have lost their vagueness, and now are well-defined. Moreover, her rather meager dress has somehow taken on dramatic color and proportion and its lines have a more expansive flow.*

With ADDIE'S *gaze on the glowing bottle, it pulsates, blinks at her and bubbles start rising—bubbles which affect its voice as it again calls, "Yoo-hoo, Addie!"*

Entranced, ADDIE *wanders over toward the bottle, the spotlight travelling with her. As she stands looking at the bottle in abject amazement,* HERMAN *notes her.*

HERMAN. What you looking at, lady?

[ADDIE *turns and looks at him, and now the heretofore unimportant* HERMAN, *moving into the spotlight, seems to tower above the bar and appears a sage and a philosopher.*]

ADDIE. [*Focusing on* HERMAN, *reacts amazed at the change in his appearance.*] Have you been here all the time?

65

HERMAN. Yes, lady.

ADDIE. [*Still peering at him.*] You look so—so interesting. Why didn't I notice it before?

HERMAN. [*Disinterested.*] Couldn't say, Ma'am. Anything you'd like?

[*Again* ADDIE *focuses on the green bottle which again says, "Yoo-hoo."*]

ADDIE. [*Vaguely indicates the green bottle.*] Please. I'll have some of that one.

HERMAN. Which one, lady?

ADDIE. [*A trace impatient.*] That one! The bottle that said "Yoo-hoo."

HERMAN. Yoo-hoo?

ADDIE. [*More impatient.*] The emerald green one that said "Yoo-hoo."

HERMAN. [*Indicating bottle.*] Cream de mint?

ADDIE. Oh, I don't care what you call it. [*Expansively.*] And you have some too! You have no idea how it makes you feel. [HERMAN *cocks an eye at her.*] You owe it to yourself.

HERMAN. Thanks, Miss. I'll take some Bourbon.

[*As* HERMAN *pours Creme de Menthe for* ADDIE *and some whiskey for himself,* ADDIE *climbs up on bar stool No. 2. She sighs.*]

ADDIE. [*Confidentially.*] D'you know what? Something must of been the matter with me when I came in here—t'night.
HERMAN. [*None too interested.*] That so?

ADDIE. Yes—when I came in here t'night, everybody seemed

like scum. But they're not like that at all. [*As she peers off at table No. 7 a spotlight centers on* BELLA *and* GABE *revealing the two in a romantic pose as lovers. Contemplating* BELLA *and* GABE, *sentimentally.*] Romeo and Juliet!

HERMAN. Huh?

ADDIE. [*Paying no attention to* HERMAN.] They're consulting with Cicero. [HERMAN *now reacts as if* ADDIE *were not only tight but coo-coo.* ADDIE *trains her gaze on* TOT *and* EMMA *whose table lights up revealing the two girls clinking glasses gaily.*] The Lorelei! [HERMAN *merely scratches his head over this one. Turning her attention to* DON *and* JUNE, *whose table No. 5 now lights up.*] Admiral Nelson and Lady Hamilton. [HERMAN *pays no more attention.* ADDIE *now looking at* PAUL, *as his table lights up.*] Him! [*She sighs—then trains her gaze on* MAUDE.] Jerk!

HERMAN. [*A word which is familiar to* HERMAN *causes him to turn.*] Did I hear you call someone a jerk?

ADDIE. [*With a gesture of infinite contempt.*] Forget her! [*Looking about,* ADDIE'S *gaze picks up* DON *and* JUNE. *She turns back to* HERMAN.] Lord Nelson. Is he really in love with her?

HERMAN. [*Philosophically.*] Could be. The one place homely girls have luck is in a saloon.

ADDIE. [*The impact of this statement causes* ADDIE *to cast a quick glance over toward* PAUL. *Then she turns back again. Revealing a budding hope.*] They do?

HERMAN. [*Having forgotten the subject.*] Do what?

ADDIE. [*Tensely.*] Plain girls have luck in a saloon.

HERMAN. Go into any saloon, Miss, and you'll see.

ADDIE. [*Deeply thoughtful.*] But isn't that because the men they have luck with are tight? [*Awaiting his answer, she watches him eagerly.*]

HERMAN. [*Giving it due consideration.*] Hm! Maybe it's because a girl that goes in a saloon ain't no square hoop. You know, they cover the territory. That's what men like.

ADDIE. Girls who take them over the horizon.

HERMAN. [*Tossing her a quick glance.*] Over the horizon. Yeah. That's what men are looking for. You said it, Miss. You sure said it.

ADDIE. [*Picks up her glass and holds it up to* HERMAN.] Here's to you, Socrates!

HERMAN. [*Sociably.*] Socrates to you too, ma'am! And all the best.

[*They clink glasses and drink.*]

ADDIE. Did I say you were interesting? Why—that isn't the word. The word's exciting. [*Looking about again.*] Everybody in here's so exciting. Nobody's scum at all with the exception of one exception. [*Her gaze centering on* MAUDE *dazedly.*] Funny! I thought she was pretty! Well—that shows the truth is bound to come out, isn't it?

HERMAN. Yeah. A few little drinks and folks look just like what you want 'em to.

ADDIE. [*Preoccupied now with* PAUL, *speaks dazedly.*] Yes. But he's just the same. [*Bristling with malice.*] So he's going to remember me next time I come into the bank, is he? Well—isn't that too nice of him? [*With a sob in her voice.*] The son of a— [*She claps her hand over her mouth.*]

HERMAN. Oh—go ahead! [ADDIE *nods her head in protest.*

Making conversation.] You may feel different about the guy when you're sober.

ADDIE. Never in a million— [*Then—with sudden pugnacity.*] Are you in-sin-u-a-ting I drink?

HERMAN. Not at all, lady.

ADDIE. [*With a mercurial. return to camaraderie.*] What's your name?

HERMAN. Herman.

ADDIE. I like you, Herman.

HERMAN. Thanks.

ADDIE. [*A moment's pause, then, apropos of nothing that has gone before, there rises to her lips a cry which states the very essence of everything that is wrong with* ADDIE.] How I wish that people loved me!

[*Her tone has so changed and her words have so much the ring of true anguish that* HERMAN *looks at her startled.*]

HERMAN. [*With a first note of interest and of sympathy shoves her drink toward her.*] Here, Sister! You better have your drink.

ADDIE. [*Using words we have heard her say in complete insincerity, now speaks them dazedly, from her very heart.*] Oh! You're sweet and thoughtful!

HERMAN. Well, Miss. I'm here to see that you're taken care of.

ADDIE. [*Even further dazed.*] Another friend!

HERMAN. What's that, Miss?

ADDIE. [*Looking awesomely over at* TOT *and* EMMA.] Yoo-hoo! Tot, dear! Emma, darling! [*They look up.*] Yoo-hoo. [*She tosses a kiss at them.*]

TOT and EMMA. [*Calling back to her as they return the kiss.*] Yoo-hoo to you, Honey! And many of 'em!

ADDIE. [*Turning back to* HERMAN, *again starts to look about, drinking in the glamour of the place and its occupants.*] This place—it's friendly and it's exciting. You feel anything could happen here.

HERMAN. [*Philosophically.*] And sometimes does.

ADDIE. I love it! A saloon is like a movie.

HERMAN. Better'n a movie maybe—'cause you're mixed up in it yourself. [*With a little laugh.*] Most of the regulars who come in here either love or hate each other. Either way, it's better than being a humdrum.

ADDIE. [*Awesomely—his remark opening up a whole new world to her.*] Why, maybe it is! Herman, you know more than all the professors that write all the books in all the whole psychology sections.

HERMAN. [*Modestly.*] I don't guess those professors get a chance to hang around a saloon much.

ADDIE. [*Vastly impressed.*] That's right! [*She picks up the Creme de Menthe, holds it toward him, then, her budding confidence giving her a sudden new inspiration, imitates the coyness of* MAUDE, *doing it gingerly.*] Well! How'd-a-doody!

HERMAN. [*Gives her a double-take—then looks at her with budding sexiness.*] Say, you're cute!

ADDIE. [*Stunned.*] It works!

HERMAN. [*Even further charmed, begins to move right in.*] What's your name?

ADDIE. [*Provocatively—trying out the brand-new attitude of a coquette.*] It's Adelaide. But you call me Addie!

HERMAN. I'm glad I met you, Add.

ADDIE. Thanky.

HERMAN. [*From his heart.*] And that ain't no bull, either.

ADDIE. Oh, thanky two times. [*Fearing she may have over-done the coquetry, she looks narrowly at* HERMAN *for his reaction.*]

HERMAN. [*Entranced—sighing.*] Don't mention it, Add!

ADDIE. [*Her heart leaping.*] My hair! It must look a perfect fright.

HERMAN. It does not! Did anybody ever tell you you're pretty?

ADDIE. No. Why—no.

HERMAN. Well, you are!

ADDIE. [*She turns to give a long and thoughtful look at* PAUL—*then—beginning to wax ambitious.*] Would you like to see me take him away from her?

HERMAN. Bet you can do it, too!

ADDIE. I can and I will. I owe it to myself. [*She opens her now vastly over-sized pocketbook and with a flourish pulls forth an over-sized dollar bill.*] It calls for music. Here's for the nickels. [*As he works the cash register,* ADDIE *waits for its musical accompaniment and, sure enough, it obliges. She sighs, delighted.* HERMAN *hands her the change.*] Thanks. [*She makes a bee-line for* PAUL, *and proceeds to "taunt" him. Speaking now as a siren.*] So you're sure you'll remember me the next time I come in the bank, Mr. Bishop?

PAUL. [*Looks up.*] Are you kidding?

ADDIE. [*With siren mystery.*] Who can tell? [*She strikes a provocative pose.*]

MAUDE. [*Speaking in the vulgar tones of the most common tart.*] Oh, go away!

ADDIE. All right! I'll go for the moment. I'll go play that record again.

MAUDE. Miss Bemis, I'll thank you to respect my headache.

ADDIE. [*En route up to juke box.*] I respect the ache, Miss Carson. [*Chuckling diabolically, she starts to put a nickel in the juke box.*]

MAUDE. [*Completely routed.*] Oh!

PAUL. [*To* MAUDE.] You better not mix it with her, Honey.

[*"Melancholy Baby" starts again on juke box.*]

JUDGE. [*Coming down to* TOT *and* EMMA.] Good evening, girls.

TOT. Hello, Pinkie!

EMMA. [*Gesturing toward chair Left of table No. 3.*] Would you like to put it there awhile, Your Honor?

JUDGE. Thanks, Emma.

[ADDIE *is now making a bee-line for them.*]

TOT. [*To* JUDGE.] How is your poor skinny wife?

[*They all laugh and* ADDIE, *hearing them, is attracted and goes toward them.* BELLA *and* GABE *come down to dance floor and start dancing.*]

ADDIE. My friends! Are you having fun?

TOT. Your Honor, meet Miss Bemis—she's a real live wire.

ADDIE. Oh, Tot, thanks! [*She pumps the* JUDGE's *arm.*] Judge, your client, Bella and I, we're an old neighbor.

JUDGE. You mean Bella Lane?

ADDIE. Yes! So, I'm terribly interested. Will he be able to get his divorce before she gets her baby?

[BELLA *and* GABE *look over, annoyed.*]

EMMA. [*Studying* BELLA *with interest.*] Baby! Pinkie, you do get the juiciest cases.

JUDGE. He can't afford a divorce, Miss Bemis.

ADDIE. Poor little Bella!

TOT. Yes, she loved not wisely but too soon.

BELLA. [*Turning to* ADDIE.] How would you like to mind your own business?

ADDIE. Bella! You're in trouble, aren't you?

GABE. Well keep it under that hair-do of yours, Sister, will you?

ADDIE. [*Coming around to* BELLA *and* GABE.] Of course I will. Bella, when we lived next door we weren't very close. But I've a bank account—a secret bank account. Nobody knows anything about it, and if it'll help it's yours to see you through. Every penny of it.

GABE. Do you really mean that?

BELLA. She's had too much to drink. Come on, Gabe. [*Turning away.*]

ADDIE. [*Following them around.*] I've got my checkbook with me. All you have to do is say the word.

JUDGE. The word is two hundred and forty-three dollars and eighty cents.

ADDIE. You've got it!

[GABE *and* BELLA *stop dancing; turn to* ADDIE.]

GABE. Well, holy smoke!

TOT. Didn't I tell you she was a sugar-pot.

BELLA. And I always thought you were an empty night-gown.

GABE. [*Shaking* ADDIE's *hand.*] Put it there, Addie! You're a champ if I ever met one.

ADDIE. Another friend!

GABE. I bet you got a million.

ADDIE. I've got a start.

JUDGE. If you ever need a divorce, miss, come to me.

ADDIE. [*Turning to* JUDGE.] Oh, thanks for the compliment. [TOT *starts to sing "For She's a Jolly Good Fellow."* OTHERS *join in, including* ADDIE. *To* MAUDE *and* PAUL *as she notices them.*] I don't need you! I've got friends to protect me. Lots of them. And I haven't even started. [*She looks about, counting her friends on her fingers and ends by noticing the solitary* GIRL *at the bar. Seeking new worlds to conquer she makes a bee-line for* GIRL.] Honey, you look as if you didn't have a friend in the world. What's the matter?

GIRL. Nothing. [*But her manner of saying it reveals something is very wrong indeed.*]

ADDIE. Why are you in here all alone?

GIRL. [*Dejectedly.*] I didn't notice you come in with any Shriner's Convention.

ADDIE. [*Watches her compassionately a moment—then tries again.*] Do you come often to the Jersey Mecca? [*The* GIRL *nods.*] Alone? [GIRL *nods.*] Why do you do it? Tell me. Won't you?

GIRL. [*Bursting out emotionally.*] Will you please go away?

ADDIE. [*Completely thoughtless of the recent disposal of her bank account.*] Look! If something's wrong that could be helped by money, I've got some saved up in a bank. [*The* GIRL *looks up.*] You can have it all, and welcome every penny of it.

GIRL. [*Amazed.*] Well, thanks! Gee, that's swell of you. But money can't help me. I've just been feeling sort of lonesome. That's all. [*Tears starting to well up.*] Today's my birthday.

ADDIE. Your birthday! [*She shakes her head in sympathy.*]

GIRL. But it's her birthday, too. Seventy million men in America and I have to fall for a guy whose wife's birthday is the same as mine.

ADDIE. Tsch! Tsch! Tsch!

GIRL. [*The flood gates now open wide.*] Oh, it isn't only birthdays I'm alone. It's every holiday. I've never watched the New Year in with Waldo or looked at fireworks on the Fourth of July. I've never had turkey with him on Thanksgiving. We've never hung up our stockings together—because he has to be with her—with her and the folks.

ADDIE. [*From her very heart.*] I'm so sorry!

GIRL. [*With mounting pathos.*] They even have fun on St. Patrick's Day—even on April Fool's they play jokes on each other. [*Cheering up a trace.*] I'm a Baptist, so I don't mind much when they celebrate Yom Kippur.

ADDIE. [*In sudden inspiration.*] D'you know what? I'm going to give you a birthday party!

GIRL. [*Unable to believe her ears.*] A birthday?

ADDIE. Yes, my friend. Right now! If it takes every penny in my bank account.

GIRL. [*Completely bowled over.*] Gee, but that's sweet of you!

[ADDIE *gives the* GIRL *a slap on the back of hearty camaraderie so violent as to cause her to jump, then turns and starts Right for the door. As* ADDIE *goes, the* GIRL, *vastly cheered, primps and fixes her makeup for the birthday party. En route,* ADDIE *looks off for* GAIL *and bumps into* DON *as he is headed to put a nickel in the juke box.*]

ADDIE. Oh, Mrs. Hosmer. Beg pardon. [*As* DON *starts to brush past her,* ADDIE *suddenly stops him.*] A hero! I salute you! [*She proceeds to do so.*]

DON. Do I fascinate you?

ADDIE. A hero! And a prospective friend!!

DON. [*Grinning.*] Say—you've had your eye on me all evening.

[*Now* JUNE *moves into the light.*]

JUNE. [*To* ADDIE, *jealously.*] Lady, I smell something burning, and it's me.

ADDIE. [*To* JUNE.] You're beautiful! [*She puts two of their hands together and presses them warmly. Then her tears near to the surface.*] Bless you. Bless you both!

JUNE. [*Relaxing.*] Why, aren't you sweet! Thanks, Sister.

ADDIE. Don't mention it, Sister! [*Then thrilled—with a start.*] Now, I've even got a sister! [*Then expansively.*] I'm giving a party. Will you two come to it?

DON. [*To* JUNE *delightedly.*] A sucker!

[JUNE *laughs and pulls him up stage.*]

ADDIE. Oh, thanks. [*Striking an attitude, addresses the whole roomful.*] Attention, everybody! I want to make a little speech.

[*Cheers from* ALL.]

MANUEL. Bravissima!

[*At which point* GAIL *breezes up Left. She appears extraordinarily lovely and gracious.*]

ADDIE. [*Dazed at the change in her.*] Mrs. Hosmer!

GAIL. [*Turning to beam on* ADDIE.] Yes, Miss Bemis.

ADDIE. Call me Addie, won't you, Mrs. Hosmer?

GAIL. Call me Gail, child.

ADDIE. [*Moving down Center.*] Child! Now I've got a mother!

TOT. [*Piping up.*] Dolling, did you mention something about a party?

ADDIE. A party? Oh!—Oh, yes. A birthday party! [*Turning toward* HERMAN.] D'you know what that means, Howard?

HERMAN. [*In correction.*] Herman.

ADDIE. [*Taking the correction in stride.*] Herman, it means champagne! [*Striking an attitude.*] Enough champagne for everybody in here!

[ALL *cheer.*]

MANUEL. Bravissima!

ADDIE. Bravissima!

HERMAN. D'you want a magnum, Addie?

ADDIE. [*Recklessly.*] I want a magnassimum!

EMMA. She's a sweetheart!

[HERMAN *proceeds to open wine and pour it.*]

GAIL. [*Graciously, but with a modicum of concern.*] Isn't that a rather extravagant order for you, Honey?

ADDIE. [*Wallowing in barroom camaraderie.*] Nothing's too extravagant for my friends. [*With a sudden glance toward*

PAUL, *she gets an idea. Sits at table with* TOT *and* EMMA.] Here! I have my check book. [*She moves a check book from her purse which, magically, is about- twice the size of the purse itself.*] Will you summon my banker to come to me please.

GAIL. You mean Paul Bishop?

ADDIE. That's it. And tell her this time he's got to come because it's business.

[*As* GAIL *starts to cross toward* PAUL, DAD *approaches* AD-DIE.]

DAD. Take it easy, Addie! Your father was around not long ago.

ADDIE. [*Startled.*] He was?

DAD. I made him go 'way—but he could come back. And if he caught you making a play for Mr. Bishop, he'd—

ADDIE. I wouldn't touch him with a pole foot ten.

PAUL. [*After reluctantly leaving* MAUDE, *now approaches.*] Yes, Miss Bemis?

ADDIE. Mr. Bishop! I'll beg you to trouble for the fountain pen.

PAUL. Here you are.

ADDIE. [*As she writes check.*] Don't be presumptuous. This is merely business. Will you merely tell Gail this check of mine's all right.

PAUL. [*With reservation.*] For how much, Miss Bemis?

ADDIE. For merely fifty dollars!

PAUL. [*His tone indicating that fifty is about her limit, turns to* GAIL.] Yes—that's okay, Gail.

ADDIE. [*Rises. As she gives the fountain pen back to* PAUL, *switches to sexiness and fairly coos.*] There you are. Thanky.

PAUL. [*With an embarrassed laugh.*] Don't mention it.

ADDIE. [*To* DAD, *as she gives* PAUL *a sexy little pat.*] My banker! [*With great dignity as she waves the check to* GAIL.] And my check!

GAIL. Thank you, dear.

DON. [*As* DAD, HERMAN *and* GLORIOUS *start to pass around the champagne.*] Step up, folks. Here comes the giggle water.

OMNES. Ah! Champagne!

HERMAN. [*Crossing Center. To* ADDIE, *as he presents her with a glass of champagne.*] Here, Addie! [*Raising a glass of champagne.*] Here's to you, Add. May all your troubles be little ones.

[*He treats her to a big, sexy wink which* ADDIE *returns with two-fold sexiness.*]

ADDIE. And may all your little ones be yours!

JUDGE. [*Calling to her.*] How about that speech, Miss Bemis?

OMNES. [*Ad lib.*] That's right! Let's have a speech, dear! Speech! Speech!

ADDIE. [*Applauding herself, as she heads for bar.*] Speech! Speech!

[*At which, realizing she is out of order, she starts to mount stool No. 2 at the bar. She continues to mount the stool, with some hazard now, for the stool's legs are beginning to lengthen. The* OTHERS *cheer her on. By this time* ADDIE'S *stunt has caused everyone to react with an admiring suspense. And now, with the stool's legs at least double their normal length, she gains a cocky equilibrium and sits down as the stool begins to rock from side to side. She finally obtains its balance, and strikes an attitude of triumph. Her audience relaxes and breaks into ardent applause. Heard above it is:*]

MANUEL. Bravissima!

ADDIE. Bravissi-missima! [*High above her audience in this ideal spot from which to enter the speech-making phase of her toot,* ADDIE *looks about, savoring the fruits of popularity, and finding them sweet beyond belief. Finally with a gesture, typical of the ham speech-maker, she holds her hand up for the applause to cease, which it does, right on the dot. Now becoming very elaborately serious,* ADDIE *clears her throat. In the best traditions of pompous speech-making.*] Ladies and Gentlemen! Brother'n and Sister'n and Mother'n. [*This last to* GAIL.] My friends! [*Pausing to give her words further weight, she looks about.*] I want to tell you how much real joy it gives me to be among you on the birthday of a friend who is very close to my heart. [*Waxing very mellow.*] —Very close. [*Turning to* GIRL.] What's your name, dear?

GIRL. Myrtle.

[*A laugh begins to merge from* ADDIE'S *audience, but she quickly holds up her hands, and on the dot it ceases. Then—*]

ADDIE. [*Assuming the ham speech-maker's attitude of pomposity.*] It's Myrtle's birthday! [*As* MYRTLE *rises to take a bow, the applause switches directly to her. Annoyed at losing her spot as center of attraction.*] Myrtle, sit down! [MYRTLE *sits.*] Why should we pin ourselves ex-exclusively to Myrtle's birthday? Anybody can have a birthday—anytime they feel— [*This giving her a new inspiration, she breaks off and starts afresh.*] Why, it was only tonight, under these very portals, that I was born all over. Happy birthday to me!

OMNES. [*Ad lib as they applaud with fervor.*]

TOT. And many of 'em!

EMMA. All the best!

JUDGE. Hear! Hear!

GAIL. Happy birthday, Honey!

DON. You're okay, babe!

BELLA. Many of 'em, Addie!

ADDIE. [*She stops the applause, then with the gesture of a radio master of ceremonies coaxes them on. Then stops them, then a second time coaxes them on and stops them. She then becomes serious and very mellow.*] And now I'd like to take this opportunity to pay tribute to the National Bank of Newark where Mr. Paul Bishop is doing such an outstanding job at window number three.

[*They all applaud and* PAUL *is forced to rise and bow.* ADDIE *looks at him lost in a daze. There is a pause.*]

TOT. [*Calling to* ADDIE.] Go on with your speech, Duckie!

EMMA. Get down to the toast, dear. I'm thirsty!

HERMAN. Here, Addie, fill up your radiator.

ADDIE. [*Snapping out of it.*] Oh, yes. Ladies—and gentlemen! To Mildred!

GIRL. [*Piping up.*] It's Myrtle.

ADDIE. [*Shooting* MYRTLE *a look.*] Correction! To Myrtle and Myrtle's birthday—the one holiday that belongs only to her— [*With* ADDIE'S *gaze on* MYRTLE, MYRTLE *shifts uneasily, which brings her plight to* ADDIE'S *mind.*] —with the exception of a certain married woman, who shall be nameless. [*Addressing* MYRTLE.] May your birthdays last as long as you live.

GIRL. [*Beaming.*] Gee! Thanks!

OMNES.

GABE. You said it!

MANUEL. Bravissima!

DON. Now you're talking!

GAIL. You're going great, Honey!

HERMAN. That's the stuff, Add.

BELLA. Good for you, babe!

GLORIOUS. Hallelujah!

MYRTLE. Gee—thanks a lot!

JUNE. That's it, kid!

MARGOT. Ole! Ole!

TOT. We love you, dear!

EMMA. You're an ace, Honey!

ADDIE. [*Now climbing up on the bar.*] To friendship! And the place where it is born. The Jersey Mecca! [*Her gesture taking in the whole place. They* ALL *drink.*] And to think when I came in here tonight, I thought it was a dump! [*Ad lib, as they laugh.*] I didn't realize it was Fairyland. [*Awesomely.*] Better than Fairyland.—It's Hollywood! [*At which the entire set goes Hollywood, lights up to its limit and reaches the apex of glamour. The music swells and bubbles start to rise from above the bar—bubbles which assume the size of toy balloons.*] With which few brief remarks, I close my speech for the evening. [ADDIE *suddenly dives right off the bar, luckily being caught by* HERMAN *and* GABE. GAIL *now approaches* ADDIE *with her change.*]

GAIL. That was a lovely dive, Addie.

ADDIE. [*Archly—making a joke.*] So is this!

GAIL. [*Laughing.*] You've got a fast line, Addie. Here's your change.

ADDIE. Thanky, Gail dear. And now—

[*At which point* DON, *who has been consulting with* MARGOT *and* MANUEL, *takes the mike in order to make an announcement.*]

DON. Look folks—this party hasn't even started! Margot and

Manuel are giving us a little preview of their novelty Bull
Fight Samba!

ADDIE. [*With no intention of being overlooked.*] But wait a
moment! I'm not through yet. I'm going to buy some more
champagne.

DON. Take it away, Margot and Manuel.

[BERT *plays piano. The dance is already starting and nobody
pays her any attention. She critically looks the dancers over.*]

ADDIE. Who's giving this party anyway?

HERMAN. Here, Addie—some more champagne.

[*The beginning of the number consists of* MARGOT *sitting
alone at table No. 5, absorbed in her drink.* MANUEL *circles
the table as if he were a stranger on the make while* MARGOT
pretends disinterest.]

MYRTLE. Sit down, Addie, we can't see.

[ADDIE *wanders diagonally across dance floor, behind* TOT
and EMMA, *then down near phone.*]

EMMA. [*To* TOT *in comment on* MANUEL.] Sexy, ain't he?

[TOT *sighs entranced. At which point* ADDIE *starts jealously
to move in on the act.*]

ADDIE. [*Speaking as a means of drawing attention to herself.*] Bravissima!

EMMA. [*Beckoning to* ADDIE.] Ssst, Addie! Come sit with
us, Honey.

[*But* ADDIE *refuses the invitation. As the dance continues,*
ADDIE *looks up at the lily.*]

ADDIE. Hello, Lily. [*The lily pays her no attention.* ADDIE
shrugs. MANUEL *now leans across the table and, fixing his*

eyes on MARGOT'S, *proceeds to "hypnotize" her. Then slowly he moves back, luring* MARGOT *with hypnotic gestures while* MARGOT, *her eyes still "fixed" on his, rises in the manner of one hypnotized and slowly follows* MANUEL *to the dance floor where, never taking her eyes from his, she whips off and tosses aside her large circular rumba skirt, disclosing a scant under-dress of shorts.* EVERYBODY *applauds, except* ADDIE, *and they proceed to go into their dance.* ADDIE, *trying to attract attention to herself.*] I can do that, Mr. Bishop.

[*The number is a novelty—a "bull fight tango" in which* MARGOT *uses her skirt as a bullfighter's cape. As the dance progresses* MARGOT, *or* MANUEL, *holds the skirt out as does a matador in his "come on" to a bull.*)

PAUL. [*With Babbit-like enthusiasm in the number.*] Say— this is swell!

ADDIE. [*Noting* PAUL'S *enthusiasm,* ADDIE *starts to imitate* MARGOT. *Calling to* PAUL.] Oh, Mr. Bishop! Look.

[PAUL *neither sees nor hears her and* ADDIE, *in order to force his attention slides right into the cape, fastens it about her waist and starts giving all.*]

DAD. [*Trying to catch* ADDIE's *eye.*] Addie! Oh, Addie.

ADDIE. [*Hears but pays no attention and starts posturing around with a little more emphasis, moving in on floor.*] Look, Mr. Bishop, I'm dancing!

DAD. [*Now going to* ADDIE.] You're getting in the way!

MARGOT. [*Withdrawing from routine.*] Leave her alone.

[ADDIE *takes her place.*]

GAIL. It's all in fun, Dad.

DAD. I keep thinking of her old man!

GAIL. Oh! That's right. Yeah. [*To* ADDIE.] How about a ringside seat, Addie?

ADDIE. Look, Mr. Bishop! [*With which she starts to give a very special wriggle of the hips.*]

DON. [*Calling to* ADDIE.] Shake it, Sister. You're tops.

MARGOT. [*Amused, applauds* ADDIE *from the sidelines.*] Ole! Ole! Ole!

ADDIE. [*Over her shoulder to* TOT *and* EMMA.] Is he looking?

TOT and EMMA. Yes, sure!

ADDIE. [*Giving instructions to piano player.*] Tango!

[*The samba music stops and slow tango music begins as* ADDIE *swings into it with* MANUEL *in the manner of a professional. Her audience is most enthusiastic.*]

PAUL. Say! She's good.

[ADDIE *reacts to praise then—to* MANUEL, *indicating she wishes to be raised up—*MANUEL *raises* ADDIE *and, as they all applaud, she kisses her hand to* PAUL. *Then dismissing* MANUEL *she dances over to* PAUL *and takes his hand.*]

DAD. [*To* GAIL.] Now this *is* dangerous!

GAIL. [*Reassuringly.*] Keep an eye on the door.

[DAD *proceeds to do so and* ADDIE *increases the intensity of her attack on* PAUL.]

MAUDE. [*With sarcasm.*] The life of the party, isn't she?

GIRL. [*Speaking up.*] Scared of losing him, dear?

[MAUDE, *forced to disclose her lack of jealousy, gives* PAUL *a nudge.*]

MAUDE. Dance with her, darling. Go on!

[*And now* PAUL, *half in "party" mood and half embarrassed, gives in sheepishly to* ADDIE'S *hypnotic advances, proceeds to join her and take her in his arms, at which* ADDIE, *tossing aside every vestige of restraint, starts giving all. Their spectators, by now in the full spirit of fun, applaud* ADDIE'S *every wriggle, while* BERT, *watching as he plays, grins and begins to add to the corn of her performance by kidding the music. Presently* DAD, *dividing a worried interest between* ADDIE *and the door, gives a start as it opens. He relaxes on seeing the newcomer is not* BEMIS *but a swarthily handsome gentleman of about thirty-eight, who appears worried— flustered. It is* NANINO, *who on emerging from glass enclosure crosses Center, stands looking about.*]

TOT. [*Gesturing with her thumb toward* NANINO.] S-s-st, Emma! Pipe! He looks Eyetalian. Could he be—?

EMMA. Might be! [*Studying him with awe.*] Gee—what a physique he's got.

TOT. Yeah! And every ounce of it is Latin.

[*At which point* NANINO *spots* MAUDE *and makes a bee-line for her.*]

EMMA. Sure, it's him! Watch this!

TOT. Yeah! It's going to be rich.

[*By which time* NANINO *has gained* MAUDE'S *table and* MAUDE, *whose rather "bored" interest has been on* PAUL, *now sees him.*]

MAUDE. [*Giving a little start. She rises.*] Vittorio!

NANINO. [*With accusation.*] When I heard you were down here I said well I'll be damn fooled.

MAUDE. [*Amazed.*] You heard I was— [*Sits.*]

NANINO. Yes. What are you doing?

[*He now sits in* PAUL'S *chair above table.* PAUL, *glancing over, sees him and, wondering who he is, watches narrowly.* ADDIE, *absorbed in dancing, pays no attention.*]

MAUDE. [*Noting* PAUL'S *gaze on her, grows more frightened.*] I—I— It was lonesome at the flat.

NANINO. You shouldn't come places like this alone. It don't look nice.

MAUDE. You—you can't expect me to spend every night in that lonesome flat.

NANINO. [*Gives her hand a proprietory pat.*] I know, Bambina. I'm sorry. [*Seeing the hand-pat,* PAUL, *reacting with jealousy, tries, without any cooperation from* ADDIE, *to dance her over toward* MAUDE, *causing her fresh heart failure. He sees* PAUL'S *glass.*] Whose drink is that?

MAUDE. It—it was—you know, Clara's. She's gone. Let's go too.

[*He is relieved but refuses to budge.*]

NANINO. [*Wiping his brow a trace nervously.*] I need a drink! Waiter! I just stopped by the hospital.

MAUDE. Hospital?

NANINO. Yeah. I've got a friend who's sick.

[*With* ADDIE *retarding* PAUL'S *progress toward* MAUDE *by violently jerking him back at a point where he is at arm's length from her,* MAUDE *watches in covert suspense.*]

DAD. [*To* NANINO.] What will it be, sir?

NANINO. Double rye. [*To* MAUDE.] A Pink Lady, darling?

MAUDE. No. Nothing. [*In an attempt to escape the inevitable clash of her two lovers, rises.*] While you're having your drink, I'll just slip out to the powder room. [*She starts, surreptitiously trying to negotiate an exit into the street.*]

PAUL. [*But seeing her, calls out.*] Where you going, Honey?

[NANINO *turns. Caught in her attempt to escape,* MAUDE *stops, trying to make herself as small as possible.*]

ADDIE. [*To* PAUL, *as she pulls him further away from* MAUDE.] Oh—let her go.

NANINO. [*Rises.*] Is that man annoying you?

MAUDE. No. He's—he's just—

PAUL. [*Louder and more insistent.*] Honey, who's your friend?

[*Gulping,* MAUDE *hesitates, not knowing whether to continue to go back or what.*]

NANINO. He's trying to pick you up. You shouldn't come to places like this without me.

PAUL. [*Trying to get away from* ADDIE *who, completely and deliriously absorbed in hanging on to him, pays no attention to anything else. Crosses to* MAUDE.] She's here with me, sir.

NANINO. [*Flaring up.*] With *you?* [*Jerking* MAUDE *back.*] Come back!

ADDIE. [*To* NANINO.] Who invited you to the party? Go home!

PAUL. [*To* ADDIE, *trying to pull himself free of her to get to* MAUDE.] Please, Miss Bemis. [*Pushing her aside.*]

NANINO. [*To* MAUDE.] Who is that guy?

MAUDE. It's—it's—

EMMA. She's flirting with death!

TOT. Yeah! It's lovely.

PAUL. Will you leave this young lady alone? It happens we're going to be married.

NANINO. Married?

ADDIE. [*To* NANINO.] Will you go home!

NANINO. [*To* MAUDE.] Who is he?

MAUDE. [*Cornered.*] Mr. Bishop, meet Mr. Nanino.

ADDIE. [*Suddenly catching the name,* ADDIE *gives a joyous start and, starting to applaud.*] Welcome to Mr. Nanino! [*Singing the name "Nanino! Nanino! Nanino!" over and over, dances solo with an increase of high spirits.*]

NANINO. [*Smouldering—turns on* MAUDE.] So that's why you're stalling on that switch to Park Avenue?

PAUL. [*Speaking up.*] Maude should have told you, Mr. Nanino, but since she didn't, we're turning in her resignation now.

NANINO. Resignation?

PAUL. [*To* MAUDE.] What are you to this guy?

[*At which point the telephone starts ringing and* DAD *goes to answer it.*]

MAUDE. I'm—nothing.

NANINO. [*Hurt to the quick.*] Nothing? Bambina!

[*Simultaneously.*]

PAUL. Why can't an em-
ployee quit you, Mr. Nanino?
[*Suddenly whipping about to*
MAUDE.] Or are you some-
thing more?

MAUDE. [*Aghast at the idea.*]
Of course not.

[ADDIE *stops dancing and
watches, worried, over a possible capitulation from* PAUL.]

DAD. [*In phone.*] Hello.—
Yeah. This is Jersey Mecca.
—Who.—I didn't catch you,
lady.—Oh.—Well, just hang
on a minute. I think the guy's
here. [*To* BERT.] Shh! [*The
music stops.*]

PAUL. [*To* NANINO.] Will you try to get this through that
dumb head of yours? She's getting married.

[ADDIE *deflates.*]

DAD. [*Turns toward* NANINO.] You're Mr. Nanino, aren't
you?

NANINO. [*With a sudden start.*] Yes!

DAD. It's the hospital—wants to speak to you.

NANINO. [*Excitedly.*] Hospital!

ADDIE. [*To* TOT *and* EMMA.] Hospital!

NANINO. [*To* PAUL.] You wait here. I want to talk to you.

[*He rushes to the telephone.*]

ADDIE. [*To* TOT *and* EMMA.] He wants to talk to`him! [*She
laughs her diabolic laugh.*]

NANINO. [*In telephone.*] Hello. Hello. Miss Monahan? Any
developments?

PAUL. [*To* MAUDE *in bitter accusation.*] "Bambina"!

MAUDE. He didn't mean it like that.

NANINO. [*With increasing agitation.*] It is? I'll be there right away. [*He starts to hang up—then speaks again.*] Give Mama congratulations. Goodbye. [*He hangs up, then—in a panic to leave—crossing to* MAUDE. *Gets hat and coat.*] I'll be at the flat in an hour. See that you're there. [*Starting for door.*]

MAUDE. [*Who has been reacting with suspicion during the telephone talk, swoops to stop him.*] Where are you going?

NANINO. [*Manly pride breaking through all his other emotions.*] To the hospital. My wife! She's just had a boy!

[EVERYONE *responds.*]

MAUDE. [*Revealing, in spite of herself a deep affront.*] Vittorio! You said your wife didn't understand you.

PAUL. Maude!

NANINO. You go to the flat. I go to the hospital to see my boy. Then I see my wife. Then in one hour I see you.

ADDIE. What a man!

NANINO. [*Turns, sees her, and speaks in the exuberance of joy over his fatherhood.*] Thank you, Miss. Well, good night. [*He exits.*]

MAUDE. [*Turning to* PAUL.] Paulie. Take me home. [*Dazed* PAUL *turns away, down Left. Following him.*] Paul! You don't understand. About Mr. Nanino! Or Hollywood! Or anything. I've only been trying to get some sort of—of security—to depend on myself because—because every man who falls in love with me gets tired of me in a little while.

PAUL. [*He stiffens.*] Yeah?

MAUDE. Maybe you think I've done wrong, Paul! But if I did—it's because I—because it doesn't mean anything to me to—to let somebody—hold hands—or something. It isn't my fault if I don't feel things, is it? Is it?

PAUL. [*Ashamed for her.*] Be still, Maude!

[*He crosses Right.* MAUDE *follows. Fearful* MAUDE *can square herself,* ADDIE *watches narrowly.*]·

MAUDE. Paulie! I know I was stand-offish with you but I was afraid. Afraid if you got used to me, you wouldn't care about me any longer.

PAUL. [*Rather gently.*] Oh, please!

MAUDE. I'm always saying something wrong. I'm such a fool!

[*She bursts into violent, pathetic tears.*]

PAUL. [*His male heart torn by the sight of tears.*] Oh, Honey! Don't cry. Please! I'll do anything, but please don't, cry.

[ADDIE, *showing desperation, galvanizes. But, getting an idea, looks toward the mike.*]

MAUDE. That's better better. [*Feeling that she has got him winging.*] Paulie! Come on. Take me home to my place. Or, if you want, I'll go to your place and I'll make up to you for everything I have ever denied you in the past. Paulie. We'll start all over again. Only this time it'll be your way. You won't be sorry, Paulie. [*By which time* ADDIE, *in order to drown* MAUDE *out, grabs the mike and starts to sing through it, singing "I Haven't Got a Worry in the World." Not with the meagre voice of* ADDIE BEMIS, *but in her ex-*

tremity, with the colossal volume of a Flagstad. During the above we see MAUDE *gesticulating and talking, her arguments completely drowned out by* ADDIE'S *brilliant coloratura performance. The* ONLOOKERS, *delighted as always by a good healthy shindy, react with laughter and make comments which, because of the clatter caused by* ADDIE'S *performance, are mere pantomime.*] Be quiet, you little idiot, you're drunk. [*To* ADDIE.] Shut up, shut up, I say. [*Finally screaming so as to be heard even above* ADDIE'S *singing.*] All right! Let her make a fool of me. [*Choosing to be "jealous," gets raincoat and umbrella—then back to* PAUL.] But don't ever expect me to speak to you again as long as I live.

[*Turns to door. As she whams out* ADDIE *takes a high, triumphant note and ceases singing. But suddenly* PAUL *starts out after* MAUDE.]

ADDIE. [*Swooping to him, grabs his arm.*] Mr. Bishop! Where are you going?

PAUL. I'm going to settle with that guy! I'm going to bash his head in! I'll kill him! I'll—

ADDIE. Wait! [*He looks at her.*] Say the books of the Bible.

PAUL. What?

ADDIE. The minor prophets of the Bible. Say them. It's important. [*She brings him down Center.*]

PAUL. [*Her request so takes him by surprise that* PAUL *suddenly finds himself obeying. Speaking, as per usual, in one breath.*] Hosea, Joel, Amos, Obadiah, Jonah, Micah, Nahum, Habakkuk, Zephaniah, Haggai, Zechariah, Malachi.

ADDIE. Now! Don't you feel better?

PAUL. [*Dazedly.*] Yeah. [*With deep dejection calls to* HER-

MAN.] Herman, give me a double Scotch!

ADDIE. I'll have one, too.

HERMAN. Double Scotch for little Addie!

DAD. [*Trying to stop* ADDIE.] *Addie!*

[DAD *brings the drinks. As* PAUL *starts to toss his drink down,* ADDIE *reaches out and stops him.*]

ADDIE. Wait! Let's have a toast, Mr. Bishop! [*She picks up her drink, entwines her arms through* PAUL'S *and snuggling to him in this intimate position, starts to give a toast.*] Here's to—

DAD. [*At which instant,* DAD *speaks up from doorway.*] Addie! Your father's coming in.

[EVERYBODY *galvanizes, except* PAUL, *too dejected to pay any attention.*]

DON. [*With a sadistic grin.*] Well, Mom! Here it comes.

GAIL. Oh God!

TOT. [*Rushing to* ADDIE'S *rescue.*] Get into the can, dear! Hurry.

[*But by this time* BEMIS *is lurching in and cutting off all possibility of escape.*]

JUNE. It's too late. Here he is.

TOT. [*To* EMMA *as she shields* ADDIE *and* PAUL.] Duck under that table, you two. Go on.

[EMMA *joins* TOT *and, covering* ADDIE *and* PAUL, *they start to back them toward table No. 4 down Right where they put down their drinks and crawl under table.*]

GAIL. Play something, Bert. [BERT *plays "Stars and Stripes Forever." Taking charge, she approaches* BEMIS *casually*] Good evening. Can I do anything for you, Mr. Bemis?

BEMIS. I'm looking for somebody. [*He starts to glower about the room.*]

DAD. [*Going to help* GAIL *out.*] That guy you're looking for came in here, Mr. Bemis. But he went home.

BEMIS. He ain't home. I've been there. [*Very surly,* BEMIS *goes and leans against the bar. Aware of the dangerous situation, the* OTHERS *self-consciously go about their affairs,*

GAIL, DAD *and* DON *on the alert for possible trouble. To* HERMAN.] Rye whiskey.

HERMAN. Yes sir.

DAD. [*Quietly.*] Look, Mr. Bemis. Why don't you go try some of the other places for that fellow?

BEMIS. I got a hunch he'll be coming in here. [*He tosses his drink down in one gulp—while* HERMAN *goes to replace the bottle.*] Leave the bottle!

[HERMAN *looks at* GAIL *for her attitude and* GAIL, *in a mood of "anything to gain a little time," nods for him to leave it.*]

GAIL. Okay, Herman.

HERMAN. [*Putting down the bottle.*] There you are, sir.

[*And now, with* EVERYBODY *almost having heart failure, we see* ADDIE'S *hand reach from under the table for the drinks she and* PAUL *left there, taking one of them at a time. At which point, to* EVERYBODY'S *intense relief,* ADDIE'S *hand secures the last of the two drinks and disappears. As* EVERY-

BODY *looks with suspense toward* BEMIS *who starts to pour himself a second shot of rye, the lights begin to fade and a spot centers on the table which miraculously begins to gain height. The table cloth parts as double curtains to reveal a very romantic interior, with* ADDIE *and* PAUL *seated on what would normally be the base of the pedestal but which appears to be a comfortable divan.* PAUL *is still dazed—dejected.*]

ADDIE. [*A drink in each hand, holds one of them out to him.*] Don't you want your drink, Mr. Bishop?

PAUL. Thanks.

[*He takes the glass and places it on the floor but, as he does, the utter misery written on his face stabs at her woman's heart; making* ADDIE *ashamed of her triumph and guilty over what she's done to him.*]

ADDIE. Do you feel awful about all that?

PAUL. What do you think?

ADDIE. [*A little pause—then, with deep sincerity.*] I want to tell you something, Mr. Bishop.

PAUL. [*Disinterested.*] Yeah?

ADDIE. I was the one that sent for Mr. Nanino.

PAUL. [*Looks at her.*] Sent for him?

ADDIE. Yes, I did it hoping that what happened would happen. And it happened.

PAUL. Oh, well—it had to come out sometime. I guess I knew it all along. I'm nervous. The fellows at the bank— they worry over me. I don't sleep. I drink too much. Yeah, I knew it all the time. [*He suddenly covers his face with one hand.*]

ADDIE. [*Shattered by sympathy,* ADDIE *looks at him. Finally as a cry from her very heart.*] Oh! You look just like a small red wagon that's lost his little boy! [*With infinite sympathy.*] Don't look like that, Mr. Bishop. I can't stand it.

PAUL. All through the war I dreamed of having a girl and a place of my own and kids. But it can't seem to work out. Now I'm through.

ADDIE. Maybe you'll find somebody else.

PAUL. No. Women are no good for me. I've had experience.

ADDIE. Have there been others? [PAUL *nods.*] Women like Miss Carson?

PAUL. No. They were different altogether. One was a blonde and the other, she was blonde, too, but lighter. I guess I've got to go it alone. [*Once more he buries his face in his hands.*]

ADDIE. [*Looks at him almost unable to bear his anguish. Finally: In an earnest attempt to cheer him.*] Oh! You mustn't do that, Mr. Bishop! Why, Benjamin Franklin says a man without a woman is like a half a pair of scissors.

PAUL. [*This suddenly catches* PAUL'S *interest and he looks up, laughs slightly.*] Half a pair of scissors. You're the funniest little thing I ever met.

ADDIE. Funny, peculiar, or funny to laugh?

PAUL. Both. I don't know. [*Studying her.*] First I thought you were dumb. Then you turned into a hellion. The next thing, you're a highbrow. Next thing you're giving me the come-on. Yeah. You're funny. Never a dull moment.

ADDIE. Thanky. [*Then quickly.*] I mean, thanks.

PAUL. You are funny. I can't figure you out.

ADDIE. You didn't think I'd really put it in a washing machine, did you?

PAUL. Put what?

ADDIE. Your handkerchief. I was planning to bring it back to you tomorrow from the Bemis hand laundry, all spick and span.

PAUL. Thanks. I'm not used to that kind of service.

ADDIE. But now I'd like to keep it.

PAUL. Help yourself.

[As ADDIE *reacts, her heart once more leaping, he starts to take a swig of his highball. She reaches up and stays his hand.*]

ADDIE. Wait! [As PAUL *looks down at her, she holds her glass toward him.*] Let's have a toast. [*She clicks her glass against his.*] Here's over the horizon. [*She drinks.*]

PAUL. [*Starts to drink—then desisting—looks down at her curiously.*] "Over the horizon"! [*With a little laugh.*] That comes out of that library of yours, I suppose.

ADDIE. [*Quite simply.*] No, it's out of my heart.

[As again she starts to drink, PAUL *suddenly reaches out and grabs her hand.*]

PAUL. [*Speaking roughly.*] Cut that!

ADDIE. [*She looks up at him surprised.*] Why?

PAUL. [*Bitterly.*] You don't belong in a bar, Miss Bemis!

ADDIE. I thought you said that's where men meet girls.

PAUL. Girls? That's where you meet two-timers and double-crossers. Not you.

ADDIE. Why not me?

PAUL. [*Suddenly flaring up.*] Don't laugh at me.

ADDIE. I'm not laughing at you.

PAUL. Yes you are and I don't like it. Anyone but you.

ADDIE. Why anyone but me?

PAUL. I don't know why, but you make me feel ashamed.

ADDIE. I do?

PAUL. Don't laugh at me, please.

ADDIE. [*Unable to contain her joy.*] I'm not laughing at you. I'm just laughing. [*She starts to recite.*]

> My heart it's like a singing bird
> Whose nest is in a water'd shoot;
> My heart is like an apple tree
> Whose boughs are bent with thick-set fruit;
> My heart is like a rainbow shell
> That paddles in a halcyon sea;
> My heart is gladder than all these,
> Because my love is come to me.

[*Slowly, as she continues,* PAUL *raises his face and looks at her as if hypnotized by the beauty and music of her words.*]

> Raise me a dais of silk and down;
> Hang it with vair and purple dyes;
> Carve it in doves and pomegranates;
> And peacocks with a hundred eyes;
> Work it in gold and silver grapes,
> In leaves and silver fleurs-de-lys;

Because the birthday of my life
Is come, my love is come to me.

[*Then—modestly.*] That's Christina Georgina Rossetti, 1830–1894.

PAUL. [*Awesomely.*] Gee you looked wonderful while you were saying that!

ADDIE. [*Again her heart leaps.*] I did? [*There comes over her one of those lucid intervals which sometimes emerge right in the middle of a jag. She holds up her glass and looks at it.*] Funny what drink will do, Mr. Bishop. It'll make a plain girl like me seem wonderful.

PAUL. You are wonderful.

ADDIE. [*Quickly.*] Here! Have another drink.

[*She puts the glass to his lips, but PAUL brushes it aside viciously. He takes her impetuously into his arms and kisses her with a fierce passion. As the music swells into a crescendo, the table cloth curtains fall, the lights go on full, and we are back in the Jersey Mecca*]

BEMIS. [*Is at the bar, just pouring out the last of the rye from the bottle. He tosses it off. Apparently winding up a speech.*] And I'll say it right to his face—then I'll push his face in.

HERMAN. [*Indicating the empty bottle.*] Well, you've milked this one, sir. Good night.

BEMIS. Gimme another.

[HERMAN *looks toward* GAIL *who shakes her head and now moves down Left Center.*]

GAIL. Look, Mr. Bemis! I wish you'd go home and stop

worrying about that daughter of yours. Believe me, she's perfectly capable to—

BEMIS. [*Belligerent. Turning to* GAIL.] How do you know?

GAIL. [*Flustered.*] I—I've met her.

BEMIS. Where?

GAIL. At—at the Beauty Shop.

BEMIS. [*Leaning across table toward* GAIL.] She never went to a beauty shop. She wouldn't be so frivolous. She wants to feel sorry for herself.—Down the street she goes looking so damned humble everybody says, "Look at Addie Bemis. Ain't it pathetic what she takes from her old man?" Making me seem I'm the worst guy in Newark. The worst guy in Newark! Well, I ain't. And I can't take it. And what would you do? I go out and get drunk.

GAIL. Well kids are a worry, Mr. Bemis, sure! But I can't see that's any excuse for—

BEMIS. She drives me outta my wits. Never busting loose. No guts. Never raising her voice. Making me yell at her. Turning me into a louse. Everybody is always saying, "How does that pure little sweet little Addie Bemis stand that old man of hers." Well, I'll tell you what they ought to be saying. They ought to be saying, "How does that poor old man of hers stand that pure little sweet little Addie Bemis," that's what.

DAD. [*Moves up to try to calm him.*] Take it easy, Mr. Bemis!

BEMIS. [*His voice all the louder.*] And when I get a beer for myself out of the icebox what do you think she does? Makes herself a cup of tea. And what does she tell me today? She tells me she's mashed on a guy that works at the bank—did you hear that—the bank. And you know why? That's so folks will say "Look at Addie Bemis' old man. If she wasn't tied up to him, she could be a fine lady married to the bank clerk." Well, she ain't going to get away with it. I'll fix Mr. Bank Clerk. [*At which point the table cloth of the table sheltering* PAUL *and* ADDIE *shakes a trifle, nearly causing* EVERYBODY *heart failure. However,* BEMIS *turns back to* HERMAN *and they relax a trifle.*] Gimme another.

HERMAN. That's all tonight, sir.

BEMIS. Mrs. Bank Clerk and her twenty-four dollar shoes!

GAIL. Mr. Bemis. Why don't you knock off and go home?

BEMIS. Did you ever notice her shoes? Did you? [*Turning to* HERMAN.] Where's that drink?

HERMAN. I said that's all, Mr. Bemis.

BEMIS. [*His belligerence rising.*] And I said gimme another.

GAIL. [*Turning toward* DON.] Don. [*She significantly gestures with her head toward* BEMIS.]

DON. [*To* BEMIS—*quietly*—*as he approaches.*] Don't you think you'd better run along, pal.

BEMIS. I'm not gonna leave here.

DON. Oh, I think you are. Come along now. Say nighty-night to the folks.

[*As he takes* BEMIS *by the arm, and starts him toward door, it suddenly shoots out clipping* DON *on the chin with a power which floors him.*]

GAIL. [*Thoroughly frightened, rushes to help him up.*] Don!

GABE. [*Rising to the rescue, grabs* BEMIS *by the scruff of the neck.*] Come along, Bemis. Get out of here.

BELLA. Gabe! Watch yourself.

[*At which* BEMIS *suddenly swings free, by rolling* GABE *over his shoulder onto the floor down Left. In the melee that ensues* GAIL *grabs a bottle from the bar and heads for* BEMIS, *who snatches it from her grasp and wheeling around stops all would-be oncomers. The screams of the women stop and there is deadly silence as* BEMIS *surveys the room. Squaring off belligerently, he faces all of them.*]

BEMIS. As I was saying, Mrs. Bank Clerk and her twenty-four dollar shoes! All you need for a tip-off on what she is, is take a look at her shoes, strapped around the ankles like a fancy girl. She and that damn library. A fancy girl! And pretending she's so damned highbrow she wouldn't— [*At which point he breaks off, hypnotized by the sight of* ADDIE'S *feet which protrude from under the table.*]

EMMA. Holy God!

BEMIS. [*Becoming livid.*] I'm lookin' at a pair of shoes! What's going on here?

[*And now with* EVERYBODY *practically paralyzed with fright,* PAUL'S *feet join* ADDIE'S *protruding from under the table.*]

GAIL. Folks! Take it easy. We don't want the cops here!

BEMIS. [*Lurching down Right toward table.*] Come out of there, you two! [*He gives the table cloth a jerk, which reveals* ADDIE *in* PAUL'S *arms. His voice rising.*] Come out of there!

[*Now* ADDIE *and* PAUL *break, look up, see him and react alarmed.*]

TOT. [*To* ADDIE.] Stay where you are, dear!

BEMIS. [*Grabbing* ADDIE *by the arm, jerks her out.*] I'll fix you, Mr. Bank Clerk! What are you doing under that table?

PAUL. [*Now struggling to his feet.*] Leave her alone!

[*He makes for* BEMIS *who wards him off, and shoves him past him.*]

ADDIE. Paul! Don't.

BEMIS. [*With bottle he starts with slow menace for* PAUL *who now stands stock still.*] I'll lay your head open for you!

ADDIE. You do and you'll regret it!

GAIL. I'll handle him, Addie.

BEMIS. Why, you—

[*He lunges toward* PAUL *with the bottle held above his head.* ADDIE, *who is standing in back of* BEMIS, *wrenches the bottle from his grasp and hits him over the head with a terrific blow. The bottle breaks and everyone screams.* BEMIS *falls and is dragged into a chair at the Right Center table by* GABE *and* JUDGE. *During which the telephone starts to ring frantically.*]

EMMA. [*As the commotion subsides.*] Is he dead?

JUDGE. No. He's all right.

[ADDIE *stiffens.*]

GAIL. Thank God for that!

JUDGE. [*To* DAD.] Let's have some water.

DAD. [*Relievedly—going to bar.*] Okay, Judge.

GAIL. [*To* GLORIOUS.] Answer that phone, will you, Glorious?

GLORIOUS. Yes, ma'am.

DON. [*To* GABE. *Rubbing his jaw.*] Gee! He sure packs a wallop, don't he?

GABE. I'll say! And an old guy, too.

GLORIOUS. [*Who has been saying, "Hello.—Hello, Miss Carson.—Yes, he's still here." Now turns to.* PAUL.] It's Miss Carson, Mister B. Does you want to talk to her?

[ADDIE *who has stiffened during the above, watches* PAUL *without even breathing.*]

PAUL. [*A moment's hesitation—then.*] All right.

[*As he goes to the telephone* ADDIE *watches closely.*]

[*Simultaneously.*]

PAUL. [*In telephone.*] Hello, Maude. You are? Are you? Well I don't know, Maude. Yes, Maude, but— All right. I'll be over.

JUDGE. [*Splashing water on* BEMIS.] Here, Mr. Bemis. You're all right. Just take a deep breath. That's the ticket, Mr. Bemis. Feeling better?

GAIL. All right, folks. Break it up. Get back to your tables.

[*As* PAUL *hangs up and starts for the door,* ADDIE *deflates completely, all her spirit leaving her.* ALL *return to their places except* JUDGE *who is with* BEMIS.]

PAUL. [*Suddenly remembers* ADDIE *and turns*] Oh! [*Showing embarrassment, he approaches her.*] I—I'm sorry, Miss Bemis. I guess I was a little bit—a little bit—fresh this evening. But I wish you'd be generous and forget it.

ADDIE. [*Gamely and with dignity.*] It's quite all right, Mr. Bishop. I've found out how folks behave when they've had too much to drink.

PAUL. Well, I'll look forward to seeing you in the bank sometime.

ADDIE. [*Extremely formal yet extremely gracious.*] Yes—I'll see you at the bank sometime.

PAUL. Goodbye, Miss Bemis.

ADDIE. Goodbye, Mr. Bishop.

[*At which* PAUL, *with no further ceremony, goes on out.*]

JUDGE. [*Pulling the gradually revived* BEMIS *to a sitting position.*] There he is, little lady. And no harm done.

ADDIE. [*Paying no attention, goes to* HERMAN.] I'm thirsty. Herman, fix me a Horse's Neck.

HERMAN. Addie, better leave me fix you a Prairie Oyster.

ADDIE. All right, give me a Prairie Oyster.

BEMIS. [*Groggily.*] Did she say a Prairie—

HERMAN. Yeah. She's due for a helluva hangover!

BEMIS. A hangover! [*Turning to* JUDGE.] Say, Judge! I'm hearing things.

JUDGE. No you're not. [*Turning to* ADDIE.] Addie didn't hurt you. You're as good as new.

BEMIS. [*Flabbergasted—looks up at the* JUDGE.] Addie! Was—was Addie the one that—

JUNE. [*Cutting in.*] Yeah! She hung one right on your knob, Mr. Bemis!

GABE. [*With admiration.*] And what a sock!

DON. Why, that broad's a powerhouse.

TOT. She hasn't got any guts, eh? Wait till you feel that bump on the back of your head!

JUDGE. [*Desirous of calming* ADDIE's *fears.*] But don't you worry, Addie.—He's going to be all right.

ADDIE. [*At bar.*] Well that's too bad! I wish I'd killed him.

BEMIS. [*Even more flabbergasted.*] What did she say?

ADDIE. [*Turning to him.*] I said you're a meddling, drunken, worthless lout with a sour disposition and a dumb, stupid face and I wish I'd killed you.

BEMIS. [*Suddenly coming to, notices the rumba skirt she has on. Rises and crosses toward her.*] Addie! What are you doing here? What are you doing in those spangles? What have you been doing here anyway?

ADDIE. I've been acting just like you. I've been doing just what I felt like doing. I've gotten drunk and disorderly and I loved it. I'll never do it again, but I loved it tonight. I was up in a pink balloon. And I was happy for the first time in my whole, ridiculous, little dried-up, shrivelled-up life, till you came in and ruined everything.

BEMIS. What were you doing under the table?

ADDIE. I was making love to a man, a man I hardly even know. He was kissing the face off me and I was kissing the face off him. And I found it highly satisfactory. Now you've really got something to holler about! Something to yell and scream and beat me up about. Only just you try to do it, one more time. Just you try!

HERMAN. [*Handing her empty bottle over the bar.*] Here, Add.

[ADDIE *takes bottle and starts off.* EVERYONE *reacts.*]

ALL. Don't, Add! Watch yourself!

DON. She'll do it too!

BEMIS. [*With sudden pride in* ADDIE.] Let her go, folks. I wouldn't touch a hair of her head. That's my daughter. [*Sits Right of table No. 3.*]

[*They* ALL *relax.*]

ADDIE. [*A revelation coming over her.*] Why, Pop!

GLORIOUS. [*Singing—in warning.*] Somebody's knocking at your door, somebody's knocking at—

[*The* POLICEMAN *enters and* EVERYONE *is frozen with apprehension.*]

POLICEMAN. [*Moving in.*] So you're having trouble again, Mrs. Hosmer?

GAIL. It's nothing, Officer! Just a little family argument.

POLICEMAN. [*Seeing* BEMIS—*crosses to him.*] Hello, Bemis!

BEMIS. [*Without looking up.*] How do you do?

POLICEMAN. What are you doing here?

BEMIS. Just having a sociable little drink with my daughter. That's all.

POLICEMAN. Yeah! [*Looking at* ADDIE.] Well, she seems to be a chip off the old— [*At which point he breaks off, agape.*] Well, look who's here. Say, I'll be damned. [*He laughs.*]

ADDIE. [*Gingerly.*] Hello, Mr. O'Farrell!

POLICEMAN. Hello, Miss Bemis!

BEMIS. [*To* ADDIE.] How do you know him?

POLICEMAN. [*To* ADDIE.] I don't suppose you'll be reporting this brawl. I'll be damned.

ADDIE. Go ahead, Mr. O'Farrell. Tell them who's 6een report-ing the Jersey Mecca to the police.

[*There is a moment's silence while they* ALL *react in out-rage.*]

DAD. Addie! That's why you kept pumping me about what went on in here.

BEMIS. Addie!

EMMA. A stool pigeon!

TOT. A copper! [POLICEMAN *turns and glares at* TOT.] Beg pardon, Mr. O'Farrell.

GAIL. So it was you!

ADDIE. Yes, Gail, it was me. [*She sits other side of table No. 3 from* BEMIS.]

DON. [*Deeply contemptuous.*] Well—would you ever think it? A canary!

DAD. But look, Gail! It was only on account of her father—that's what she—

ADDIE. Yes, I was worried about my father and— No! That wasn't it. That was only an excuse. I hated this place. [*Rises—crosses Right.*] I used to walk by here and look in the window and see girls laughing and talking with fel-lows and— No, that wasn't it. It was anybody that was doing anything that I couldn't do. I hated Scarlett O'Hara. I threw that book clear across the library floor one day because I couldn't bear to think of— No, that wasn't it. [*Crossing Left toward bar.*] It was when I was at home playing that damn piano and singing those songs to myself and I knew that someplace some girl was dancing with some fellow to that tune— [*Turning Center.*] No, that wasn't it.

[*Sits in same chair as before.*] It was Paul Bishop—with those bars that stood between us in the bank teller's window. This evening it started raining—and I knew he was coming here—and it rained and rained—and then I put on my best suit and my new hat and I— Gail! I have a headache.

GAIL. [*Still bitter.*] There's no reason to inform on folks because they're trying to have a little fun.

ADDIE. I know—I guess it's hard to understand anything— yourself or anything—unless you've gotten close to other people.

[GAIL *doesn't comment.*]

BEMIS. Drink your Prairie Oyster, Honey, and I'll take you home. [*As* ADDIE *picks up Prairie Oyster,* BEMIS *turns to* EMMA. *Indicating Prairie Oyster.*] I don't find them very helpful myself.

EMMA. Personally, I belong to the "hair of the dog" school.

BEMIS. So do I. Maybe it's better, Addie, if you just come home and make yourself a cup of tea.

GLORIOUS. [*Gets coat from rack.*] Here's your coat, Miss Bemis.

ADDIE. [*Rises as she gets into it.*] Thanks.

GAIL. [*To* POLICEMAN.] How'd you like to get yourself a cup of coffee in the kitchen, Officer?

POLICEMAN. Thanks. Don't mind if I do. [*He exits up Left.*]

ADDIE. [*Starts for door—then notices rumba skirt.*] Oh—I forgot. The party's over. [*Taking off skirt.*] Thanks, Margot. [*She turns back toward* GAIL *as the telephone rings.* GLORIOUS *answers it.*] Goodbye, Gail. Goodbye, Myrtle. Come on, Pop. [*She turns and starts for the door with* BEMIS *following.*]

GLORIOUS. [*At telephone.*] Hello. [*Big grin.*] Yes, she's still here. [*She turns to* ADDIE.] It's for you, Miss Bemis.

ADDIE. [*Looking up in amazement.*] For me?

GLORIOUS. [*Beaming.*] That's what I said, Miss Bemis.

ADDIE. [*Going to telephone.*] Hello.—Oh hello, Mr.— Yes, I'm still here.— Why, yes, Mr.— Why, y-e-s. All right. Goodbye. [*She turns from telephone. To* BEMIS.] Pop, would you mind going home, alone? I've got a date.

BEMIS. [*Amazed.*] A date!

ADDIE. Yes! I've got a date.

GAIL. Honey! Do you mean it's—?

ADDIE. Uhm-hum!

DON. Say—did he call you up from that redhead's apartment?

ADDIE. No. [*Crossing Center.*]

DON. Oh—she threw him out, eh?

ADDIE. He never even got there.

JUNE. Where'd he call up from, dear?

ADDIE. [*Crossing Left at table No. 2.*] The cigar store on the corner. [*Sits chair Right of table No. 2.*]

BEMIS. Well—guess I'd better get on or I'll bump into him. So long, Addie. [*Crosses Right; turns.*] Don't stay out too late.

ADDIE. Hurry up, Pop, go on.

[*Motions him away—he exits.*]

EMMA. Here, Honey! Try my lipstick, this time. It stands up much better under wear and tear. [*Crosses to* ADDIE.]

ADDIE. Thanks.

TOT. [*Crossing to* ADDIE.] Have a few drops of my perfume, Addie. It's called Vooley-Voo. That's French, dear, for "Help yourself to the bacon."

JUNE. [*To* HERMAN.] Say, Pal—have you got an aspirin? Maybe it'd help her headache.

ADDIE. Headache's gone.

GAIL. Get back to the piano, Bert. Scatter, everybody; you look like you were in a grandstand.

[*They scatter and wait. And wait.*]

HERMAN. If that was me I'd be here by now.

ADDIE. [*With sudden inspiration.*] Oh!

[*Quickly she rises, switches over to* MAUDE'S *chair, seats herself, crosses her legs and takes a pose which is partly the pose of a siren and partly the pose of a Queen—but altogether the pose of a woman who knows that she is loved.*

Finally PAUL *enters. As he walks toward* ADDIE *the stage begins to light up with a pink glow which emanates, this time, not from alcohol in* ADDIE'S *brain, but from love in* ADDIE'S *heart.* ADDIE *pretends not to see* PAUL *until he starts to take his seat. Then she looks up at him. They exchange a self-conscious smile. The music rises triumphantly.*]

THE CURTAIN SLOWLY FALLS

CPSIA information can be obtained at www.ICGtesting.com
Printed in the USA
BVOW081632100113

310178BV00011B/1051/P

9 781258 324261